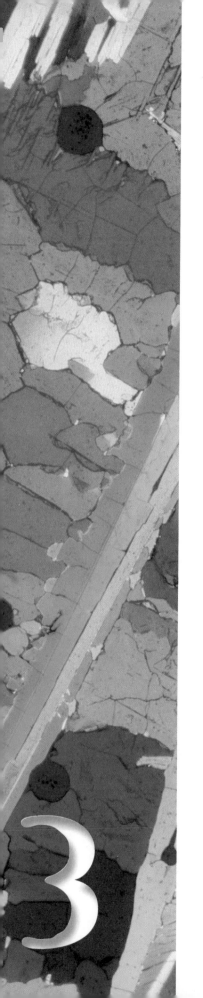

English Frameworking

The creative literacy course for English at 11–14

Julia Strong
Deputy Director, National Literacy Trust
Pam Bloomfield
Kim Richardson

National Literacy Trust
Building a literate nation

Published by HarperCollins*Publishers* Limited
77–85 Fulham Palace Road
Hammersmith
London
W6 8JB

www.**Collins**Education.com
On-line support for schools and colleges

British Library Cataloguing in Publication Data
A catalogue record for this publication is available from the
British Library.

Acknowledgements

The publishers gratefully acknowledge the following for
permission to reproduce copyright material.

Text: Extract from 'This Fella I Knew' from *Walking the Dog*
by Bernard MacLaverty, published by Jonathan Cape. ©
Bernard MacLaverty 1994. Reprinted by permission of
Rogers, Coleridge & White Limited, 20 Powis Mews, London
W11 1JN. All rights reserved (p18). Extract from 'A Woman
of No Standing' by Brendan Behan from *After the Wake*
published by The O'Brien Press Limited. © Brendan Behan,
reprinted by permission of the publishers (p21). Extract from
'The Welcome Table', from *In Love and Trouble* by Alice
Walker published by The Women's Press. Reprinted by
permission of David Higham Associates Limited (p25). 'The
Verbs in English Are a Fright' by R. Lederer from *Crazy
English* published by New York Pocket Books 1990.
© R. Lederer. Reprinted by permission of the author (p30).
Extract from *Notes from a Small Island* by Bill Bryson,
published by Transworld Publishers, a division of The
Random House Group Limited. © Bill Bryson. All rights
reserved. Reprinted with permission (p32). Extract from
www.epa.gov. Reprinted with permission (p53). Extract from
www.eduweb.com. Reprinted with permission (p61). Extract
from Socialist Alliance general election leaflet (Streatham).
Reprinted by permission of Dave Franklin (p82). Extract from
Pygmalion by George Bernard Shaw © The Public Trustee as
Executor of the Estate of George Bernard Shaw 1957.
Reprinted by permission of The Society of Authors on behalf
of the Bernard Shaw Estate (p86). Extract from *Our Day Out*
by Willy Russell, published by Heinemann Educational. ©
1976 W. R. Ltd. Reprinted by permission of Casarotto
Ramsay & Associates Limited (p91). Listings extract from *The
Big Issue (South West)* no. 453 (3-9 Sept 2001) © The Big Issue,
South West. Reprinted with permission (p97). Extract 'Should
there be a ban on hunting?' by Jerome Monahan from The
Guardian, 16 January 2001. © Jerome Monahan. Reprinted
with permission of *The Guardian* (p103). Extract from
www.peevish.co.uk from 'A Dictionary of Slang'. Reprinted
with permission (p105). 'Rising Five' by Norman Nicholson
from *Collected Poetry*, published by Faber and Faber Limited.
Reprinted by permission of the publishers (p109). 'This Is
Just to Say' and 'The Red Wheelbarrow' by William Carlos
Williams from *Collected Poems Volume 1* published by
Carcanet Press. Reprinted by permission of the publishers
(p113). 'According to My Mood' by Benjamin Zephaniah
from *Talking Turkeys* (Viking 1994). © Benjamin Zephaniah,
1994. Reprinted by permission of Penguin Books Limited

(p114). 'Twelve Songs IX' by W. H. Auden from *Collected
Poems*, published by Faber and Faber Limited. Reprinted by
permission of the publishers (p118). 'Long Distance II' by
Tony Harrison, from *Selected Poems* published by Faber and
Faber 1995. Reprinted by permission of the author (p119).
'Death of a Naturalist' by Seamus Heaney from *Death of a
Naturalist*, published by Faber and Faber Limited. Reprinted
by permission of the publishers (p121).

Photos: John Walmsley, pp5, 129, 144; Corbis, pp19, 29, 55,
113; Mersey Ferries, p33; National Theatre, pp39, 40, 45, 85,
89; Mary Evans Picture Library, p42; Bridgeman Art Library,
pp43, 73, 117 (top 2); EPA, p53; Educational Web
Adventures, p61; BBC, pp67, 71; Conservative Party, p77; PA
Photos, pp83, 101; Michael Trench, p99; Photofusion, p103;
Faber Publishers for the cover of *Serious Concerns* by Wendy
Cope, p107; Tony Stone, p109; The Museum of Modern Art,
p117 (bottom); P.J. Arkle, pp129, 139; Holmfirth Web, p135.

Cover and internal design by Ken Vail Graphic Design

Commissioned by Helen Clark

Edited by Angela Wigmore and Kim Richardson

Picture research by Gavin Jones

The publishers would like to thank Rachel Orme-Smith
for her outstanding editorial contribution to
English Frameworking.

Production by Katie Morris

Printed and bound by Scotprint, UK

Whilst every effort has been made both to contact the
copyright holders and to give exact credit lines, this has not
proved possible in every case.

Internal artwork by Janek Matysiak, pp9, 127, 147; Andrew
Clark, pp11, 13; Jennifer Ward, pp17, 31; Paul McCaffrey,
pp23, 95, 142.

NLT website
www.literacytrust.org.uk

Contents and skills matching grid

Section	Page	Word level	Sentence level	Text level		Speaking and listening
				Reading	Writing	
Reviewing Year 8 and looking forward to Year 9	5	**2, 3**, 6	1, **7**	3, 13	1, **3**	1, 4, 10
Imagine, explore, entertain	17	1, **3**, 4, 5, **7**	4	6, 9, 11, **16**, 18	**5**, 6, 7, 11, 17	**2**
● Writers from various cultures	18					
● Literary non-fiction (travel writing)	28					
Inform, explain, describe	39	**3**, 4	**7**, 8, 11	1, **2**, 4, 8, 14, 15	4, **9**, 10, 11, 12	**13**
● Shakespeare play	40					
● Media texts (websites)	52					
Persuade, argue, advise	63	8	**3**, 4, 5, **6, 7, 9**	**7**, 10, **12**, 15	4, 12, 13, **14**, 15	3, 5, 6, **7, 9**
● English literary heritage (Pre-1914 fiction and poetry)	64					
● Campaign literature (manifestos, letters, interviews, polemical essays)	74					
Analyse, review, comment	85	6	2, **3**, 4, 5, **9**, 10	3, **7**, 14	**9**, 10, **16**, 17	3, 11, 12, **13**, 14, 15
● Playscripts	86					
● Journalism (reviews, interviews, analysis)	96					
Plan, draft, present	107	6	**3**, 4, 5, **9**	**7**, 17	1, 2, **3**, 4, 8	1, 4, 8, 10
● 20th-century poetry	108					
● Formal essays and presentations	120					
Preparing for NCTs	129	**3**, 4		1, 5, 13, 14	1, **3**, 7, 11, 13	
● Preparing for NCTs	130					
● Looking ahead to GCSEs	144					
Glossary	151					

*Learning objectives

key objectives are in bold

Introduction

This is the third and final book in the *English Frameworking* series which aims to help you become a powerful communicator.

In this book you will read some great writing, including short stories and poetry, as well as extracts from travel writing, novels and plays. Activities around this writing focus on building up the range and depth of your own reading. You will be analysing what ingredients help make this writing so effective, as well as using some of these ingredients in your own writing.

You will also be looking at a wide range of non-fiction texts to develop your communication skills including:

- Researching a topic and creating your own website
- Analysing political propaganda and writing your own spoof political manifesto
- Trying your hand at a range of different journalistic skills.

Discussion will be central to all these activities, helping you to sort out your ideas and express yourself clearly. So you will be polishing your skills in formal presentation as well as in writing formal essays.

All this should put you in a strong position to do well in the National Curriculum Tests in May; a section of the book helps you to prepare effectively for these tests. Finally, you'll be introduced to English GCSE, which will be the focus of your English course in Years 10 and 11.

Most of all, you will be joining in a wide range of entertaining and challenging activities which will help you to develop your English skills, so that you can succeed in all subjects across the curriculum.

Introduction

By now you should be building up your expertise in identifying and explaining types of text and expanding the range and complexity of text that you can read with ease. You should be able to write in a wide range of text genres in the appropriate style, including formal and informal English. You should also have built up an impressive vocabulary for all curriculum areas, feel confident in tackling how to spell difficult words and have strategies to hand for how to spell them as well as work out their meaning. And, of course, you should be talking confidently about all these areas, listening to what others have to contribute to discussion and evaluating the usefulness of what you hear.

English in Year 9 is going to begin with some activities that strengthen all these skills.

Key aim

In this section you will:

- Build on the reading, writing, speaking and listening skills that you developed in Year 8 and plan some key targets to develop your skills this year.

To read is to soar

Aims

On these two pages you will:

- Discuss why some people have feared the power of reading.
- Draw up a list of recommended reads for students in Year 8.
- Reflect on the range of your reading and set some targets to expand it.
- Reflect on your strengths and weaknesses in reading, and decide on some targets for developing your reading skills.

Starter as a class

To read is to soar – to fly to a point of vantage.

A journalist wrote this in a review of a book by Alberto Manguel called *History of Reading*. Think about this image for a moment. If you can read, you can rise above everything that human beings have written in all cultures over the centuries. You have access to all the great stories and all the great ideas as well as vast banks of information; you can select what interests you and widen your interests. Reading opens up innumerable doors for personal development and enjoyment.

Over the centuries many societies have tried to stop their workforces from being educated – from learning to read. For example, in Cuba in the mid-19th century the tobacco rollers banded together to hire a reader to read to them and make the day less boring. They selected the stories they wanted to hear and soon developed favourites. They got to know some of these stories by heart and started using this knowledge to crack the code of reading. When the employers realized that their workforce was beginning to become literate, they banned the readers. On 14 May 1886 the political governor of Cuba issued the following law:

1. It is forbidden to distract the workers of the tobacco shops, workshops and shops of all kinds with the reading of books and newspapers, or with discussions foreign to the work in which they are engaged.

2. The police shall exercise constant vigilance to enforce this decree, and put at the disposal of my authority those shop owners, representatives or managers who disobey this <u>mandate</u>[1] so that they may be judged by the law according to the gravity of the case.

[1] *law, decree*

Why do you think the employers may have wanted to prevent their workers from learning to read?

Introduction *on your own*

Your teacher will give you a grid (**Worksheet 1**) to fill in. Highlight the categories of text that you read and use the space beneath each category to give examples of books that you have read within this category. If what you read isn't covered on the grid, add it in the 'Other' section. Use your reading journal to help you.

ovels and short stories				
orror tories	Science fiction	Detective/ mystery	Romance	Classics/ all-time greats
	Lois Lowry 'The Giver'			Greek myths

as a group

Working in groups with similar reading interests, work out the top ten texts that you would recommend to this year's Year 8. Consider your target audience and try to include some variety, recognizing that there will be a wide range of interests. Add to your list up to five specialist interest recommendations – these may well be related to hobbies. Draw up your list like the one below:

Top ten texts
General recommendations
1 J.K. Rowling, 'Harry Potter and the Goblet of Fire'

Specialist interest recommendations
1 Debbie Sly, 'Riding a Horse'

Be prepared to present your recommendations to the class: each group member should take part in the feedback.

Have groups come up with similar lists or are they significantly different?

Development *on your own*

Quickly list what you think are your key strengths and weaknesses as a reader. Now look at **Worksheet 2**, which includes the sort of reading skills that examiners look for. Fill in the grid as honestly as you can and use it to decide which areas you need to focus on to improve your reading skills.

Plenary

What key texts or experiences would you include in your own 'History of Reading'?

The ingredients of text

Aims

On these two pages you will:

- Analyse the main features of the six key non-fiction text types and narrative.
- Review the terms that are useful for analysing language.
- Evaluate your ability to write for a range of purposes and audiences and plan your writing targets for the year.

Starter  as a group

By now you have developed significant skills in reading and writing a wide range of texts. You should also be aware of the key ingredients of the various text types and how these different ingredients can be combined to make any text fulfil its particular purpose effectively.

You will be given a wide range of terms relating to all the different types of text (**Worksheet 3**). But each group will be given only one text type to focus on. Your task is to sort the terms into two categories, depending on whether they are appropriate to your given text type:

- *Typical ingredients*
- *Not typical ingredients.*

Use the question mark if you are unsure. Be prepared to explain your selection to the class.

Introduction as a group

Your group will now be given an example of the text type that you have been allocated (**Worksheets 4a–b**).

1 See if you can find examples of all the terms that you have selected in the *Typical ingredients* category and highlight or annotate the text accordingly.

2 Now see if any of the terms you placed in the *Not typical ingredients* category can be found in this text and mark up your text accordingly.

3 Are there any other terms you think you need in order to describe the key structural and stylistic points of this text? If so, add them to notes on your text.

4 When you have finished, decide on the key points you want to make about the text and annotate the OHT of the text that your teacher will give you so that you can present your ideas to the class. Look at the example on page 9 to help you. Every member of the group should take part in the presentation. Decide who is going to explain which points and rehearse your presentation. Be prepared to answer questions on your presentation.

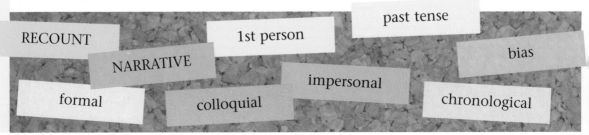

RECOUNT
NARRATIVE
formal
1st person
colloquial
past tense
impersonal
chronological
bias

NARRATIVE

autobiographical style: author writes in **persona** of the narrator

subordinate clause

<u>My father's family name being Pirrip</u>, and my christian name Philip, my infant tongue could make of both names nothing longer or more explicit than Pip. So <u>I called myself Pip</u>, and came to be called Pip. I give Pirrip as my father's family name, on the authority of his tombstone and my sister – Mrs. Joe Gargery, <u>who married the blacksmith</u>.

1st person

retells events

persona a character or role taken on by someone

Listen and watch carefully while each group presents their text. Consider whether you agree with how they are analysing their text. Be prepared to question the presenters on their ideas.

While you are listening, reflect on your ability to write in each of the writing styles being presented, in preparation for determining the targets you need to set yourself to improve your writing.

Development on your own

Use **Worksheet 5** to evaluate your writing skills. Reflect on your ability to write in the full range of writing styles. Think back to the writing skills you developed last year and the related targets that you set yourself at the end of the year. Fill in the grid, indicating which areas of your writing you feel confident about and which areas need to be improved. Use this grid to help you plan your writing targets throughout the year, as well as to help you decide on your three most immediate writing targets.

Plenary

Which of the text types causes you most difficulty as a writer? Are there any particular ingredients that cause you problems?

Spelling and vocabulary across

Aims

On these two pages you will:

- Devise an activity that will reinforce the understanding and spelling of key terms from a curriculum area.
- Help your group solve problems and evaluate alternative ideas.
- Review your strengths and weaknesses as a speller and decide what strategies will help you improve your spelling.

Starter as a group

By now you will have built up a significant vocabulary of specific terms for every subject area. The more familiar you are with these terms the better you will be able to understand, read, use and spell these words appropriately. First see how good you are with some vocabulary related to geometry.

Your teacher will give you 23 words and five headings (**Worksheet 6**), which are all related in some way to these words:

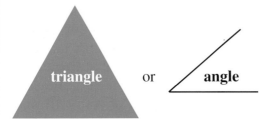

triangle   or   angle

Place the words under the most appropriate heading (see below). There are at least three words for each heading.

Link: begin with tri (contain 3 of something)

Link: a triangle has 3

Link: are all types of angle

Link: are all types of triangle

Link: all contain angles

Be prepared to feed back your group's conclusions. What is the link between the word 'triangle' and the word 'angle'?

At the end of the lesson you may be asked to spell some of these words. What strategies can you suggest to spell the more difficult words?

Introduction as a group

Your task now is to see if you can devise an activity like the one you have just been doing that would help Year 8 students reinforce their understanding and/or spelling of the vocabulary they will need for one area of the curriculum. Your teacher will provide each group with a subject area to focus on and a list of 25 related words (**Worksheet 7**). You may add or omit as many words as you want to suit your activity, as long as the new words relate to your curriculum area. You will be given some card and paper to use in your activity if you need it for the game you devise. Use your whiteboards or a piece of paper to draft your ideas.

You may find some of the following suggestions useful:

- Think up headings under which some of the words could be grouped.
- Work out how they could be sequenced (sort into a logical order).
- Link pairs for meaning or spelling.

the curriculum

P. E.

gymnastic

muscle

control

mobility

agility

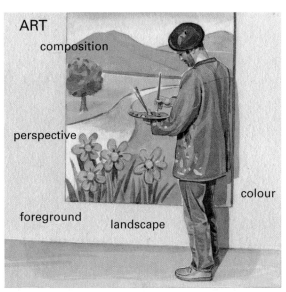

ART

composition

perspective

foreground

landscape

colour

Once you have decided on your activity, make the appropriate cards or materials to support the activity and trial them to make sure your activity works. Try to analyse why your activity would be useful and consider any problems that you think are connected with it. Be prepared to present your ideas to the class.

Make sure that you can spell the words in your subject area, as you will be tested on some of them at the end of the lesson.

Development *as a class*

Each group will now be asked to present their ideas to the class. If you haven't finished devising your activity, just present your ideas so far and the problems that you encountered. Listen carefully and decide which activities you think would work best.

Discuss which of the activities were the most effective and what qualities made them work. You may want to present the best of the activities to the relevant department in your school.

Plenary

Your teacher will now test you on 20 of the words you have been focusing on today. Be prepared to discuss which strategies work best to help you spell these words.

homework

Add to your spelling log the correct spellings of any of the words that you misspelt in the test. Focus on these words plus any other words that you have recently added to the log from any work that you have done in any subject area. Analyse why these words cause you problems and try to devise strategies to get them right in future.

Now look at the spelling strategies outlined in your spelling log and write a brief statement summing up which strategies you think work best for you and which types of words you think cause you spelling problems. Include any suggestions you have for getting them right in future.

The alibi challenge

Aims

On these two pages you will:

- Create imaginary alibis and cross-question suspects.
- Increase the speed and accuracy of your note-making skills.
- Evaluate your own skills, strategies and successes as listeners in a variety of contexts.
- Reflect on the development of your abilities as speakers and identify areas for improvement.

Starter

Can you cross-question suspects and break their alibi? This lesson you are going to play the game Alibis. Your teacher will select three people (the suspects) who have to pretend that they spent the hours of 6.00–9.00 pm yesterday together. Their task is to go outside the classroom and construct an alibi to cover their activities during this time. (An alibi is evidence proving that you were somewhere else when a crime was committed.) They must prepare to be cross-questioned on their alibi one by one.

Meanwhile the rest of the class (the prosecution) is going to focus on the type of questions to ask each of the suspects. The class's task is to prove that they have broken the alibi. This will require you to ask appropriate questions and listen very carefully to the answers given so that you can determine the most effective questions to ask next.

Discuss the following questions in pairs:

1 What would be good opening questions to begin with?

2 How could these be followed up?

3 What will you be looking and listening for as the first suspect answers?

4 When the second suspect enters, what sort of questions will you ask?

Introduction as a class

The suspects will be called in turn to be cross-questioned. Listen carefully to how each suspect answers each question and try to decide on what is the most effective question to ask next.

Try to think of questions that the suspects may not have covered but which they should know the answer to if the alibi were true. The following type of questions may prove useful:

- Was anyone sitting in front of you in the cinema/on the bus, etc?
- What did you have to eat or drink during this time?
- Where was everyone sitting in the room?
- What is the entrance to the house/flat like?
- What posters/pictures were on the walls?

On your whiteboard or a piece of paper, draw up a grid like the one on page 13 to help you focus on weaknesses in the alibi. Include any questions that caused problems, as these will be good to follow up with later suspects. Jot down any evidence that you think provides proof that they were lying.

Once all the suspects have been cross-questioned, look through your notes and put asterisks against the most significant weaknesses. See if you can place these points in order of significance.

Weaknesses in alibi		
1st suspect	2nd suspect	3rd suspect
Unsure how he travelled to house – then said walked	Hesitated, then said walked, then giggled	Tried to evade question – then said bus

Development *as a class*

Now discuss whether the prosecution has enough evidence to break the alibi. Decide which are your strongest arguments. Help your teacher establish the key evidence in order of significance. He or she will give you a key weaknesses grid (**Worksheet 8**). Note down all the evidence that you think breaks the alibi, in order of importance, and justify your selection. Keep this worksheet safe, as you will need it to help you plan your writing in the next lesson.

Now let another group create an alibi. Go through the same process. Be aware that both the suspects and the questioners will have learnt from round one. While the second group is preparing an alibi, use the time to discuss how to polish your questioning skills, considering what you learnt from questioning group 1.

Plenary

Reflect on your skills as a speaker and a listener in this context and discuss the following questions with a partner:

1 What advice would you give to a group who were about to create an alibi?

2 What advice would you give to the prosecution in how best to cross-question the suspects?

Jot down your advice on **Worksheet 8** and be prepared to share your ideas with the class.

homework

Look at your most recent speaking and listening targets. Reflect on your skills as a speaker and a listener in discussions and activities and write a brief summary of what you consider to be your strengths and weaknesses in this area. Remember to include both how you perform as an individual and when working in a group, and to include formal and informal speaking situations. End by setting yourself at least one target for speaking and one for listening to focus on this half term.

Aims

On these two pages you will:
- Write up as a formal essay what you have learnt about playing Alibis.
- Consider the effectiveness of your use of complex sentences.
- Refer back to the writing targets you have recently set yourself and see if you can meet any of them in writing your Alibis essay.

Starter

Your task today is to write this essay:

> Explain the purpose of the game Alibis and how it is played. Using one group's attempt to construct a watertight alibi, analyse what evidence there was to support the class's final judgement on whether the alibi could be broken, and what the class learnt from playing Alibis.

Your teacher will give you a number of sentence starters that could be used to write this essay (**Worksheet 9**). Sequence them in a logical order, given the nature of this essay.

- During this time, the rest of the class (the prosecution) discuss …
- In conclusion, Alibis is a good game to play because …
- Possible weaknesses to follow up with the next suspect were …
- To begin the game, the alibi group (the suspects) goes outside the classroom and …
- The class also learnt that …

- The key evidence to support this decision was …
- The group that I have selected to illustrate the game is … because ..
- By the end of the cross-examination the prosecution decided that …
- The purpose of the game Alibis is .
- By the end of this case, the class had learnt that in order to construct a successful alibi it is necessary to …
- Through interviewing the first suspect, the prosecution established that …

Be prepared to present your sequenc to the class and consider how you would write the introductory paragraph. You may be called on late to model this for the class.

Introduction as a class

Discuss the following questions:

1 The sentence starters are a mixture of past and present tense. Why?

2 All but one of these sentence starters is in the third person. Why?

3 Most of these starters form the opening to complex sentences. What is a complex sentence?

4 What is the purpose of this essay What text type is it, or does it include more than one text type

Your teacher will ask for a volunteer to model how to begin writing this essay. Be prepared to contribute you suggestions for how best to begin the essay. Make sure that the introduction includes effective complex sentences.

Development (on your own)

Look at your writing targets for this half term (**Worksheet 5**). Reflect on what you need to do in this essay to move towards achieving these targets.

Now it is time to start writing your essay. Use the structure that you created in the starter activity to help you. If you like, you can use these sentence starters, or you can devise your own. You have also got the notes that you worked on last lesson to help you. Think carefully about which tense and person to use for the different sections of this essay and how you are going to connect your ideas.

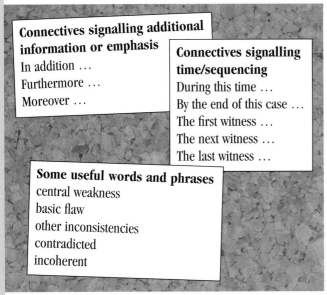

Connectives signalling additional information or emphasis
In addition …
Furthermore …
Moreover …

Connectives signalling time/sequencing
During this time …
By the end of this case …
The first witness …
The next witness …
The last witness …

Some useful words and phrases
central weakness
basic flaw
other inconsistencies
contradicted
incoherent

in pairs

Swap your draft so far with a partner's. Annotate each other's draft with suggested improvements. Try to make three positive suggestions for how the essay could be improved. Consider the following:

- Does the essay begin with a clear relevant introduction?
- Is the structure of the essay logical?
- Are the paragraphs appropriately linked?
- Has the essay the appropriate formal tone?
- Are the sentences varied in length and structure, and do they include complex sentences?
- Are the sentences appropriately punctuated?
- Are the tenses used appropriate?
- Is the spelling accurate?
- Is the handwriting easy to read?

Plenary

Your teacher will ask for volunteers to read out the first paragraph of their drafts. Can you identify features that are appropriate or inappropriate to a formal essay? Have complex sentences been used effectively?

homework

Complete your essay for homework, taking account of your partner's comments and the class discussion.

> **!** **Remember** to read through your work carefully. Would someone who had never played Alibis be able to understand your essay? Redraft your work, if necessary, and write a brief comment on how well you think you have completed the task. Have you used complex sentences effectively? Do you think you have made progress towards meeting your writing targets?

Reviewing what's been learnt

In this section you have reviewed your progress in reading, writing, building your vocabulary and spelling, as well as your ability to listen and speak effectively. In each of the lessons you have been considering your targets in each area.

Now is the time to refine your targets for the coming half term so that you have clear aims for improving all aspects of your progress in English. In May you will be taking your National Curriculum Tests which will measure your progress since leaving primary school.

Devising clear, challenging but achievable targets will help you make the progress you are capable of. Identify your key targets for this half term in your exercise book, as follows:

Reading
My targets to improve my reading are:
-
-
-

Writing
My targets to improve my writing are:
-
-
-

Spelling
My targets to improve my spelling are:
-
-
-

Speaking and listening
My targets to improve my speaking and listening are:
-
-
-

Imagine, explore, entertain

Introduction

The patterns of speech that English speakers use generally depend on where they were born and grew up. These speech patterns are often reflected in the writing that has been generated in the UK and throughout the English-speaking world.

In this section you will be looking at some cultural influences which have affected how we tell our stories, how we expect our stories to be told, and how we speak our language. You will also look at stories from a range of cultural traditions as well as travellers' tales about Britain and other countries.

As you think about these stories you will notice how they are structured, how language can reflect culture, how words can contain layers of meaning, and how poetic language can be used to recreate an image of a place. You will also notice how travel writing both entertains and informs the reader. Naturally, you will be experimenting with this type of writing for yourself – for example, you decide how best to construct a story about a victim or how effectively to recreate your memories of an interesting place that you have visited.

Key aims

In this section, you will:

- Look at stories from various cultures, consider the patterns of language they have used, and think about different ways to structure narrative.
- Consider the creative features of travel writing and compare travel writing from different times as well as writing your own.

Irish storytelling (1)

Aims

On these two pages you will:

- Think about how cultural tradition has influenced the language and style of an Irish short story.
- Think about the narrative approach of the story and what we learn from it about the culture being described.
- Use Standard English to explain your ideas.

Starter `as a group`

To begin this section you will look at the opening seven paragraphs of 'This Fella I Knew', a short story written by the Northern Irish writer Bernard MacLaverty (**Worksheet 10**). One member of the group should read the passage aloud to the group. Then underline any words or phrases that you think differ from the pattern of Standard English. Be prepared to feed your ideas back to the class.

Introduction `as a class`

The patterns of speech that English speakers use greatly depend on where they were born and grew up. These speech patterns are reflected in the great writing that has been generated in the UK and throughout the English-speaking world. The quality of Irish writing has been celebrated over the centuries – much of it reflects the strength of the Irish oral tradition and owes a debt to the poetical speech patterns of Gaelic, which influence how English is spoken throughout Ireland. One of the areas in which Irish writers have excelled is the short story. Listen while your teacher reads you all of 'This Fella I Knew' (continued right). Think about the language and narrative structure of the story and what makes it entertaining.

And, do you know, when he had earned his money nothing would do but he'd come bac home from England and buy himself a bit c land and put eleven cows on it.

But somebody had it in for him – for it didn't work out.

And didn't the cows get the grass-staggers and warble-fly and God knows what and he had to sell up the bit of land and go off again and concoct a scheme for bending cardboard boxes into hexago for decorated chocolates.

But he was a smart boy right enough, f he made money hand over fist at this and d'you know what I'm going to tell you – h was the boyo who came up with the idea thin bits of square sweets, each one in its brown envelope. Would you credit it?

And they became all the rage and the bosses at the factory went down on their knees when they heard he was leaving, but no – nothing would content him but to buy a farm of land he had seen advertised in the 'Dungannon Observer' just outside Gortin.

And all along, his mother had been mailing him the paper every week in England – in a brown wrapper. Wasn't that cute of her? To keep tabs on him, hoping to get him back one day.

Anyway, this time he stocked the farm with sheep and no sooner had he done it than they all got foot-rot and grooley stomach and that was him beat again – the lad had no luck whatsoever.

And it was back to the packaging. Tha what they called what he did. Packaging, by God. The kind of thing you or I would do at Christmas – for nothing extra.

And they paid him a fortune for it. He became known in the trade as 'the man who could package anything' – and when your man packaged it – no matter if it was a bar of soft shite – it became a best-seller.

And money became a plentiful commodity. In the digs he was paying that much that he could leave the light on all night without raising any hackles.

And every week he put some by and when he had enough ha'pence scraped together didn't he have a go at a bit of a farm for the third time. Serves him right, says you.

And this time it was the pigs. The fool gave up the job across the water.

And he comes back and buys a place beyond the bridge there. The Mammy'd be able to see him at half past ten Mass every Sunday from now on. He must have prayed the knees off himself or else the Mammy did. Because this time the boyo succeeds. And he starts making money hand over fist.

And buying that pink newspaper – and carrying a rolled umbrella from the house to the byre, if you don't mind, and wearing glasses even though he didn't need them – divil the bit – he could tell a full stop from a comma at the far end of the room. And having a mirror fitted to his bicycle instead of looking round like everybody else.

The difference between him and everybody else round here was packaging 'the product' – he wrapped it in cellophane and called it 'Bacon like it was before the war'.

And he sold everything but the grunt. The bacon itself, the pig's ears, the trotters, the curly tails – some said he sold the arseholes to school masters for elastic bands round the bundle of class pencils. Wasn't he the cute one too?

Bernard MacLaverty was born in Belfast in 1963. He worked as a medical laboratory technician for ten years before going to Queen's University, Belfast, to study English. He moved to Scotland and taught for several years before becoming a full-time writer.

Development as a group

Using **Worksheet 11** to help you, note down your response to the following questions. Be prepared to give your ideas in Standard English.

1 Why do you think the author chose to tell this story in the persona of the storyteller?

2 What sort of lifestyle do you think the narrator is used to?

3 What do you learn about Northern Irish cultural traditions from this story?

4 What does the storyteller think about the mother in the story?

5 Which phrases or sentences that the writer has used do you think are most effective?

6 What features make this story entertaining?

Plenary

How can you tell that this story was written from within a particular cultural tradition?

Add 'This Fella I Knew' to your reading record.

Irish storytelling (2)

Aims

On these two pages you will:

- Think about how cultural tradition has influenced the language and style of another Irish short story.
- Think about the narrative approach of the story and what we learn from it about the culture being described.
- Use Standard English to explain your ideas.
- Make use of a different kind of dictionary.

Starter *as a group*

Languages that develop without being significantly influenced by other languages tend to have one word for each concept, but languages – like English – that have grown up with a whole range of influences often develop many alternative words for the same thing. The foundation of English is Anglo-Saxon but many words have Latin-, Greek- or French-based alternatives. The variety of word origins means that there is a need for a thesaurus for English, a reference text that is unknown in many languages.

Some countries, for example France, have set up official organizations to protect their language and stop new words from other languages creeping into popular use. The *Académie Française* has fought a losing battle against Franglais such as *le week-end*. The British, on the other hand, seem to have welcomed a whole range of useful words into the language.

You will be given a set of cards containing a range of words, some of them slang, that have become integrated into general English from other countries, cultures and dialects – plus their places of origin (**Worksheet 12**).

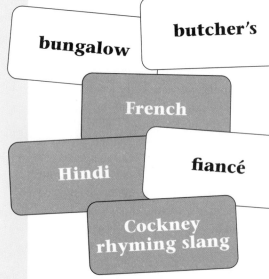

bungalow

butcher's

French

Hindi

fiancé

Cockney rhyming slang

In your groups, see if you can match up each word with its place of origin. Once you have tried your best, test your decisions by looking up the words in a dictionary, though you may need a specialist dictionary for the slang words.

Be prepared to feed back your ideas.

Introduction *on your own*

Listen carefully while your teacher reads you 'A Woman of No Standing' by Brendan Behan. (The story begins on page 21 and continues on **Worksheet 13**.) Listen carefully to the rhythm of the speech patterns in this story and think what you learn about the narrative persona that the writer has created, the culture he is describing, and who the writer wants the reader to sympathize with.

A Woman of No Standing

'And the priest turns round to me' says Ria, 'and says he: "But you don't mean to say that this person still goes to see him?"'

'"I do, Father."'

'"And brings him cigarettes?"'

'"Not now, Father, not cigarettes, he's gone past smoking and well past it, but a drop of chicken soup, though he can't manage that either, these last few days."'

'"Well, chicken soup or cigarettes," says the priest, "what really matters is that this person continues to visit him – continues to trouble his <u>conscience</u>[1] – continues as a <u>walking occasion of sin</u>[2] to stand between him and heaven. These Pigeon House people must be, shall be, told straight away. They'll be informed that you, and you only, are his lawfully wedded wife, and that show is only – what she is. Anyway, this way or that, into that <u>sanatorium</u>[3] she goes no more."'

'You know,' puts in Maire, when Ria had finished, 'it's a known thing and a very well-known thing, that a person cannot die while there's something not settled in his conscience. That one going to see him so, outside of the insult to Mammy here, his lawful wife, not to mind me, his only daughter, for all we're away from him since I was five – on the top of all that she was doing his soul the height of injury, not to mind holding his body in a ferment of pain, below on this earth, down in that Pigeon House.'

'But no matter,' says Ria, 'the priest wasn't long about seeing the Reverend Mother and leaving strict instructions that she wasn't to be let in any more – that she was no more his lawful wedded wife than the holy nun herself.'

'So now,' said Maire, 'if you don't go down early tomorrow you'll not see him at all, because I doubt if his struggling spirit will back away from <u>Judgement</u>[4] any more, now that all is settled, and his mind at ease.'

---

[1] *sense of moral correctness*
[2] *sinful person*
[3] *hospital*
[4] *God's judgement*

Brendan Behan was born in Dublin in 1923. When he was 16 years old he was first arrested and imprisoned for complicity in acts of terrorism. He then began to publish poems in Irish and stories in English. His plays, including the autobiographical *Borstal Boy*, made him known internationally. He died in 1964.

Development as a group

Your teacher will divide you into eight groups and allocate one question below to each group. Note down your key points and related evidence.

1 Is the opening of the story effective?
2 At what point does the reader know that this definitely is a first-person narrative?
3 Exactly what do we learn about the narrator from this story?
4 Approximately how long ago did Ria's marriage break up?
5 What makes the dialogue in the story effective?
6 What impression do we get of the Catholic religion from this story?
7 Who does the writer want the reader to sympathize with?
8 Is the ending of the story effective?

Feed your ideas back to the class in Standard English and see whether you agree with other groups' conclusions.

Plenary

How can you tell that this story was written from within a particular cultural tradition?

Add 'A Woman of No Standing' to your reading record.

Layers of meaning

Aims

On these two pages you will:

- Read 'Stench of Kerosene', analysing the structure of the story and considering Amrita Pritam's perspective on her culture's rejection of a childless woman.
- Explore how a writer can imply meaning through their choice of words.
- Consider how the author's standpoint can affect meaning.
- Discuss the text using Standard English, sharing ideas and accounting for differences of view.

Starter as a class

You are going to read 'Stench of Kerosene', by the Indian writer Amrita Pritam, a tragic story from the Indian subcontinent (**Worksheets 14a–c**). Listen carefully while your teacher reads the story and see if you can note how seemingly unimportant details take on deep significance as the story develops. In particular, think about how the writer has constructed this story and what message she is trying to convey.

Introduction as a group

The story begins with the arrival of the mare from Guleri's father's house to take her on her annual trip to her parents' village. The story frequently flashes back to past events to provide insight into the significance of what is happening. Your teacher will give you 18 cards for each group to sequence to show the structure of the story (**Worksheet 15**). Place the cards in the order of events in the story using the bottom row to show the events that happen in chronological order and the top row to indicate the points when the story flashes back in time.

Below is a range of significant points within the story which you will be given on cards (**Worksheet 16**). Place each card next to the paragraph or sentence which best sums up each of these points. Be prepared to explain your ideas to the rest of the class in Standard English. If you do not agree with another group's ideas, be prepared to explain why and see whether the class can reach a general agreement or can find evidence to support different viewpoints.

- The story is positive up until this point.
- The reader now understands why the Chamba fair is significant to both husband and wife.
- The reader now understands that Guleri and Manak cannot communicate, though the reader does not, as yet, know why.
- The reader realizes that Manak will not oppose his mother even though he wants to.
- The reader first understands why Manak is so upset.
- The reader realizes how strong Manak's sense of guilt is at deserting the wife whom he loves.
- The reader is now certain that the baby will not reconcile Manak to his new wife.

Development as a class

Many of the points that Amrita Pritam is making in this story only become clear when you reflect on the significance of earlier passages as new light is thrown on them. Your teacher will ask a range of questions relating to this aspect of the story. Remember to make your contributions in formal English.

1 What is the significance of using a word like 'stench' in the title of a story?

2 Early in the story, when Guleri is trying to understand why Manak is cross, Manak starts to say 'My mother ...' but then fails to complete his sentence. Later in the story, what meaning does the reader understand from this?

3 How is the significance of the flute built up throughout the story?

4 Near the end of the story, Manak's friend says he is going to Chamba for the fair. These words are said to pierce 'through Manak's heart like a needle'. How has the writer built up these layers of meaning?

5 This story focuses on the common cultural tradition of rejecting childless women. In this story, who are the victims of this tradition?

6 In the story, who is most determined to maintain this tradition?

7 What is the author's perspective on this tradition?

8 Amrita Pritam has chosen the narrative perspective of the **omniscient author** to tell this story. Why do you think she chose this?

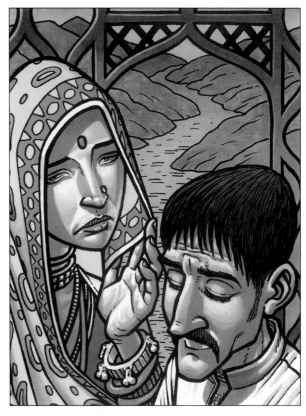

Plenary

What techniques has the writer used to pack so much significance into so small a space?

homework

Add 'Stench of Kerosene' to your reading record. Reflect on what short stories, novels or poetry you have read that reflect other cultures. Your teacher will provide you with a range of suggested reading to select from. Choose at least one of these to read and add it to your reading record.

omniscient author a narrative voice in which the author writes from the godlike perspective of knowing everything about the characters' innermost thoughts and feelings as well as all the events of the story

Insight into prejudice

Aims

On these two pages you will:

- Read 'The Welcome Table', analysing the structure of the story and considering the author's perspective on society in the southern states of America at the time the story is set.

- Explore the different layers of meaning implied by the writer's choice of words.

- Consider how the narrative voice affects the meaning of the story.

- Discuss the text using Standard English, sharing ideas and accounting for differences of view.

Starter

You are going to read 'The Welcome Table' by the American writer Alice Walker. The opening is reproduced on page 25 and continues on **Worksheets 17a–b**. Listen carefully while your teacher reads the story. Think about what techniques the writer has used to paint a picture of the great divide that has built up between the races in the story. In particular, consider how the writer has constructed this story and what message she is trying to convey.

Introduction

Discuss the following questions about the story's significance and jot down your key points. Be prepared to discuss your ideas with the rest of the class. Remember to present your ideas in Standard English.

1. The story begins with five lines from a **spiritual**. Why do you think Alice Walker chose to begin the story in this way?

2. How does the significance of the phrase 'welcome table' develop as the story progresses?

3. Why do you think the writer decided not to give the old woman a name?

4. In paragraph six (see **Worksheet 17b**), why has the writer chosen to focus in detail on what the white female church goers were wearing?

5. How do we know that the church officials and congregation did not feel guilty about turning away the old woman?

spiritual a Black American religious song

as a class

Most stories contain cultural references which add depth and meaning to the story. The second paragraph of 'The Welcome Table' (see the top of **Worksheet 17a**) is full of levels of meaning that become clearer once you have read the whole story and understand its context better.

As a class, re-read the paragraph carefully. Discuss all the possible meanings and significance of the varied references in this paragraph and be prepared to annotate a copy of this paragraph to bring out its significance.

THE WELCOME TABLE

for sister Clara Ward

I'm going to sit at the Welcome table
Shout my troubles over
Walk and talk with Jesus
Tell God how you treat me
One of these days!

Spiritual

The old woman stood with eyes uplifted in her Sunday-go-to-meeting clothes: high shoes polished about the tops and toes, a long rusty dress adorned with an old corsage, long withered, and the remnants of an elegant silk scarf as headrag stained with grease from the many oily pigtails underneath. Perhaps she had known suffering. There was a dazed and sleepy look in her aged blue-brown eyes. But for those who searched hastily for "reasons" in that old tight face, shut now like an ancient door, there was nothing to be read. And so they gazed nakedly upon their own fear transferred; a fear of the black and the old, a terror of the unknown as well as of the deeply known. Some of those who saw her there on the church steps spoke words about her that were hardly fit to be heard, others held their pious peace; and some felt vague stirrings of pity, small and persistent and hazy, as if she were an old collie turned out to die.

Alice Walker, a highly acclaimed African-American author, was born in 1944 in Georgia in the USA. During the 1960s she was actively involved in fighting for the rights of black people in America. Her best-known book, *The Color Purple*, won the Pulitzer Prize for fiction and has been made into a film.

Development as a group

Each group will be allocated one paragraph to focus on. Your task will be to re-read your paragraph carefully and draft two sentences which sum up the focus of the paragraph. Be prepared to present your sentences to the class. First, listen carefully while your teacher models how to draft a sentence to sum up the first paragraph of the story. Then, as a class, decide jointly on the sentence summing up paragraph 2.

as a class

Listen carefully as each group presents the sentences that sum up their paragraph. Ask yourself whether they have selected a sentence that sums up the essence of their paragraph effectively and be prepared to offer alternative suggestions. Together, see if the class can devise a flowchart that sums up the story.

> **Opening paragraph:**
> An old unnamed black woman dressed for church stands on the steps of a church, arousing a range of fears in the white onlookers.

Plenary

1. Why do you think that Alice Walker decided to write this story from the perspective of the omniscient author?
2. What do you think her purpose was in writing this story?

Add 'The Welcome Table' to your reading record.

Selecting your perspective

Aims

On these two pages you will:

- Explore different ways of opening, structuring and ending narratives and experiment with narrative perspective.
- Think about what spelling strategies may be useful for helping to spell commonly misspelt words.

Starter

A Year 8 student has recently misspelt the following 20 words and entered them in their spelling log. What advice can you give them about how they might be helped to remember these words? Be prepared to feed back your ideas.

although	pollution
author	recipe
beginning	seize
chronological	separately
criteria	siege
geological	sincerely
graffiti	solution
innovation	specification
meteorological	they're
parliament	whether

- Do any spelling patterns emerge?
- Are there related words that may help?
- Where would a mnemonic be useful?
- Are easily confused words causing a problem?
- Is the student checking their work carefully?

Introduction on your own

The authors of the first two stories you have read in this section chose to write in an autobiographical style, while the next two writers chose the perspective of the omniscient author as the best way to tell their stories. Today you are going to be the short story writer focusing on the following scenario.

The newcomer

A 14-year-old student's first day at a new school in the UK. They have come from a very different culture. This could be another country, such as Somalia, Bangladesh, Kosovo, or a very different part of the UK, for example someone who has moved from a rural area to a big city in a different part of the country.

Inside the newcomer's head they have four major causes of worry:

1 Family problems which led to the move

2 Homesickness for the world they have just left

3 Fear that they will be treated badly by people in the new school because they are an outsider

4 Fears of being lonely and feeling ill at ease, which would concern anyone facing a new social environment.

Before you begin writing, you must decide about the following:

- Purpose: What message are you trying to convey through your story?
- Content: What is going to happen? Will there be an incident or will it just be the story of the student's fears?

Once you have decided on the purpose and content of your story, experiment with different possible ways of telling and structuring your story.

Think about what structure would best suit your purpose:

- Chronological order
- Use of 'flashbacks' to throw light on past events which are running through a character's mind
- Reversing standard structure – starting at the end and then going to the beginning to show how events led up to this conclusion
- Cyclical narrative – where the closing of the story echoes the opening of the story.

Then consider which narrative perspective would best suit your purpose:

- Omniscient author
- Autobiographical style
- **Multiple narration**
- **Stream of consciousness.**

Try out at least two different approaches. Evaluate the advantages and disadvantages of each approach. Be prepared to explain what choices you have considered and what reasons lie behind the choices you have finally made.

> **multiple narration** using an autobiographical style but telling the same story through the eyes of two or more narrators who have differing perspectives (e.g. the new student, a student who victimizes them, the class teacher)
> **stream of consciousness** telling all the thoughts inside someone's head in autobiographical style

Development on your own

Now begin to draft your story in the perspective, structure and style that you believe works best. Give your story a title which will suggest the story's purpose to the reader.

Plenary

Swap your draft so far with a partner's. Read your partner's story carefully.

- Does the story's structure help the reader empathize with the newcomer?
- Is the sentence structure and vocabulary varied and effective?
- Can the reader picture the scenes and emotions being described?
- Is there a sense of tension that makes the reader want to read on?

Note in pencil in the margin any ways in which you think the story could be made more effective and discuss these with your partner.

homework

Re-read your draft and decide how you could improve it. Now complete your draft.

> **!** **Remember** to read carefully through your work, checking that your style helps the reader to empathize with the newcomer. If necessary, improve your story and write a brief comment on how well you think you have completed the task. Make sure that all the words are spelt correctly. Add any words you had difficulty with to your spelling log.

Travellers' tales

Aims

On these two pages you will:

- Explore how travel writing can convey information in amusing ways and its potential for poetic description.
- Analyse how the author's standpoint affects meaning.
- Consider what sort of dictionary to use for highly technical language.

Starter *as a class*

Michael Palin, former member of the Monty Python team and now famous for his television travelogues, explains, 'Reading can take me anywhere, without tickets or passports or permits.' One of the reasons that so many people love reading is its ability to transport you to imaginary worlds or to the far reaches of the real world. For the rest of this section you will be looking at how travel writers have described their own and other cultures. You will also discover that travel writers often write in such an entertaining and vividly poetic manner that you may not realize how much information they have conveyed. And, sometimes, they tell you as much about themselves as they do about the places they are describing.

Listen carefully while your teacher reads you an extract from Mark Twain's *Americans Abroad* (right; it is continued on **Worksheets 18a–b**), which he wrote in 1867 as a travel correspondent for a Californian newspaper. While you are listening, decide which paragraphs are the most entertaining and which are the most poetic. How much do you learn about Mark Twain's personality, interests and views from this passage as well as about the Parthenon (the famous 5th-century BC Greek temple in Athens)?

Breaking into the Parthenon

Bad news came. The commandant of the Piraeus[1] came in his boat and said we must either depart or else get outside the harbour and remain imprisoned in our ship, under rigid quarantine,[2] for eleven days! So we took up the anchor and moved outside, to lie a dozen hours or so taking in supplies and then sail for Constantinople. It was the bitterest disappointment we had yet experienced. To lie a whole day in sight of the Acropolis[3] and yet be obliged to go away without visiting Athens! ...

We inquired of everybody who came near the ship whether there were guards in the Piraeus, whether they were strict, what the chances were of capture should any of us slip ashore, and in case any of us made the venture and were caught, what would be probably done to us? The answers were discouraging ...

At eleven o'clock at night, when most of the ship's company were abed, four of us stole softly ashore in a small boat, a clouded moon favouring the enterprise, and started two and two, and far apart, over a low hill, intending to go clear around the Piraeus, out of the range of its police ...

[1] *a port near Athens*
[2] *compulsory isolation to prevent the spread of disease*
[3] *the fortified hill in Athens, the site of the Parthenon and other buildin*

Introduction *as a group*

Any travel writing about the Greek or Roman empires is liable to be full of historical, architectural and classical references. Most of us need the help of a dictionary to understand such terms fully, but a standard dictionary will only cover the most common of such references. For more obscure references, a **specialist dictionary** will be needed.

Using the context to help you, complete the table on **Worksheet 19** by dividing the highlighted terms from the final section of the text on **Worksheet 18a** into the four dictionary categories.

Now see if you can find the terms in the dictionaries you selected and establish their precise meaning. Also see how many of these terms would be included in a complete dictionary, as opposed to a **concise dictionary**.

> **specialist dictionary** a dictionary which gives the highly technical terms relating to specialized study
>
> **concise dictionary** a dictionary which omits the more obscure terms listed in a complete dictionary

Development *in pairs*

1 Look carefully at the final paragraph on **Worksheet 18b** and decide which techniques Mark Twain has used to convey the beauty of the Parthenon. Complete the analysis grid on **Worksheet 20**.

 Annotate one copy of this paragraph with your findings and decide how you could best present your findings to the class. Include a reading of the paragraph to bring out the beauty of the language.

2 Identify the elements that help to make 'Breaking into the Parthenon' entertaining and annotate one copy of the text on **Worksheets 18a–b** accordingly.

3 What do we learn about Mark Twain and his opinion of the Parthenon from this text? What difference does this make to the meaning of the text? Be prepared to share your ideas with the class.

Plenary

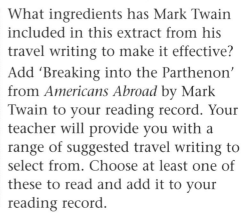

What ingredients has Mark Twain included in this extract from his travel writing to make it effective?

Add 'Breaking into the Parthenon' from *Americans Abroad* by Mark Twain to your reading record. Your teacher will provide you with a range of suggested travel writing to select from. Choose at least one of these to read and add it to your reading record.

Aims

On these two pages you will:

- Explore how travel writing can convey information in amusing ways and its potential for poetic description.
- Analyse how the author's standpoint affects meaning.
- Play with language and strengthen your understanding of the spelling patterns of regular verbs.

Starter

As soon as toddlers start learning to speak they automatically begin to become aware, without realizing it, of regular patterns within the language, such as how to form plurals and how to change the tense of verbs.

Today I walk.

Yesterday I walked.

Earlier I had walked.

When new words, like 'fax', join the language no one has to reach for the dictionary to know that the past tense is going to be 'faxed'. However, around 150 English verbs are irregular and don't follow this regular pattern.

With a partner, read the following poem about the spelling patterns of regular and irregular verbs. Can you volunteer to read it to the class in a way that will bring out the humour of the piece?

The verbs in English are a fright
How can we learn to read and write?
Today we speak, but first we spoke;
Some <u>faucets</u>[1] leak, but never loke.
Today we write, but first we wrote;
We bite our tongues, but never bote.
Each day I teach, for years I taught,
And preachers preach, but never praught.
This tale I tell; this tale I told;
I smell the flowers, but never smold.
If knights still slay, as once they slew,
Then do we play, as once we plew?
If I still do as once I did,
Then do cows moo, as once they mid?

[1] American/Canadian word for a tap

on your own

Your homework is to see whether you can write your own version of this verb poem. To help you prepare for this, you need to find a regular verb that uses the same spelling pattern as an irregular verb in the present tense. Then make the regular verb use the irregular verb's spelling pattern to form its past tense, just like the example below.

Irregular verbs		Regular verbs that have same spelling pattern in present tense		
Present	Past	Present	Past	Past (made up)
bleed	bled	need	needed	(ned)

Worksheet 21 contains examples of irregular verbs that all, in the present tense, have the same spelling pattern as at least one common regular verb. See if you can complete the grid.

Introduction as a class

Today you're going to be looking at an extract from *Transylvania and Beyond* by the Irish travel writer Dervla Murphy. In 1990, just after the fall of communism and Romania's ruthless leader Ceauşescu, she decided to travel to Romania. First she stayed in Budapest, Hungary, and set off to buy a bicycle for her trip.

Listen carefully while your teacher reads you the extract on **Worksheets 22a–b**. Think about what the passage tells you about Budapest and what style the writer has chosen to use.

Development in pairs

Discuss the following questions. You should attempt to answer all the questions but focus particularly on those that are allocated to you. You will be expected to lead the class discussion on these later. You may find it useful to annotate one copy of the extract. Use **Worksheet 23** to record your ideas.

1 What picture does the passage give you of life in Budapest? What evidence do you have to support this?

2 Re-read the following passage and see if you can work out what the highlighted words mean.

> I looked at him reproachfully, then took out my **Angol–Magyar Magyar–Angol** *utiszotar*. It listed none of those words: the nearest was *azonos* ('identical').

3 Look in detail at the second paragraph. Underline the words and phrases that are particularly effective in this section and decide what makes them effective.

4 What do you learn about the Hungarian language from this passage?

5 How is this passage structured?

6 What tone has the writer chosen to use? What evidence do you have to support this?

7 What do you learn about the writer from this passage?

8 What do you think the writer's purpose was in writing this passage? What evidence do you have to support your viewpoint?

Plenary

How has the way that Dervla Murphy has chosen to describe this incident from her travels contributed to the effectiveness of this piece of writing?

Add 'Bicycle Buying in Hungary' from *Transylvania and Beyond* by Dervla Murphy to your reading record.

homework

Use **Worksheet 21** to help you devise your own poem about regular and irregular verbs. When you have finished drafting your poem, write a comment on how well you think your poem works.

Perspectives on touring Britain

Aims

On these two pages you will:

- Read extracts from the work of two travel writers from different times and plan a grid to compare their writing.
- Analyse how the author's standpoint affects meaning.
- Explore how travel writing can convey information and ideas entertainingly.

Starter  as a class

In 1724, Daniel Defoe completed writing *A Tour Through the Whole of Great Britain*. Some 270 years later Bill Bryson, an American journalist, wrote his version of a tour around Britain called *Notes From a Small Island*. Defoe chose to open his book with a **preface**; Bryson opens his with a **prologue**. (The opening to Defoe's preface is on **Worksheet 24**; the opening of Bill Bryson's prologue is on the right.)

From their opening paragraphs you can tell that each writer set out to write very different types of travel writing. Listen carefully while your teacher reads you the two openings and decide what you can **infer** about each writer's purpose from these short extracts.

as a group

Sort out the statements you will be given from **Worksheet 25** so that they match the appropriate passage. Be prepared to support your selection with evidence from the passage.

My first sight of England was on a foggy March night in 1973 when I arrived on the midnight ferry from Calais. For twenty minutes, the terminal area was aswarm with activity as cars and lorries poured forth, customs people did their duties, and everyone made for the London road. Then abruptly all was silence and I wandered through sleeping, low-lit streets threaded with fog, just like in a Bulldog Drummond movie. It was rather wonderful having an English town all to myself.

The only slightly dismaying thing was that all the hotels and guesthouses appeared to be shut up for the night. I walked as far as the rail station, thinking I'd catch a train to London, but the station, too, was dark and shuttered. I was standing wondering what to do when I noticed a grey light of television filling an upstairs window of a guesthouse across the road. Hooray, I thought, someone awake, and hastened across, planning humble apologies to the kindly owner for the lateness of my arrival and imagining a cheery conversation which included the line, 'Oh, but I couldn't possibly ask you to feed me at this hour. No, honestly – well, if you're *quite* sure it's no trouble, then perhaps a roast beef sandwich and a large dill pickle with perhaps some potato salad and a bottle of beer.' The front path was pitch dark and in my eagerness and unfamiliarity with British doorways, I tripped on a step, crashing face-first into the door and sending half a dozen empty milk bottles clattering. Almost immediately the upstairs window opened.

'Who's that?' came a sharp voice.

I stepped back, rubbing my nose, and peered up at a silhouette with hair curlers. 'Hello, I'm looking for a room,' I said.

'We're shut.'

infer reach a conclusion from evidence, deduce

preface introduction to a text explaining its scope and intention

prologue introductory lines to a play, speech or text

32

Introduction as a class

Now listen carefully while your teacher reads you a short extract from both books describing Liverpool (**Worksheets 24** and **26**). This will prepare you for writing an essay comparing the styles of Defoe and Bryson, which you will do in the next lesson.

Your work on the openings of both books has given you some idea about the sort of differences and similarities to be looking out for. While you are listening, annotate the passages to bring out key points about the style and content of each writer. Highlight any text that supports your points.

as a group

Devise a comparison grid which will help to compare and contrast the two texts. Work out how many columns you will use and what the headings of the columns will be.

> **! Remember**
>
> - Use the statements in the opening exercise to help you.
> - Include space for quotations from the text to support your points.
> - Ensure that the order of the grid provides a logical structure for the essay.

Be prepared to share your ideas with the class. See whether the class can agree on the layout of an effective planning grid to help structure your essay.

Make a copy of the agreed grid. You will need this for your homework.

Liverpool docks

Development in pairs

One key difference between the two writers which will emerge is Bill Bryson's reliance on humour as the key way to engage his audience and convey his ideas. Highlight any parts of Bryson's account of Liverpool which rely on humour. Annotate these extracts and attempt to analyse what sort of humour he is using and what makes it effective. Be prepared to feed your ideas back to the class.

Plenary

Why is it useful to construct a planning grid?

What difference do the authors' intentions make to the meaning of their texts?

What key differences have emerged between the approaches of the two writers?

homework

Fill in the planning grid comparing the two texts. Ensure that you have identified evidence to support your points.

Comparing Defoe's and Bryson'

Aims

On these two pages you will:

- Write an essay comparing the themes and styles of Bill Bryson and Daniel Defoe, travel writers from different times.

- Integrate speech, reference and quotation effectively into your writing.

- Recognize your strengths and weaknesses as a speller and identify strategies which will help you to improve your spelling.

Starter  on your own

 Consider your own strengths and weaknesses as a speller. Using your spelling log to help you, think about which groups of words you can spell and which groups cause you problems. Now use **Worksheet 27** to help you decide which strategies work best for you and devise a plan to rectify your spelling weaknesses.

Strategy	Often use	Sometimes use	Never use	Words it has helped with
1 Break the word into sounds (e.g. e-n-t-e-r)				
2 Break the word into syllables (e.g. in-ter-est-ing)				
3 Break the word into its root and affixes (e.g. un-help-ful)				
4 Use a mnemonic (e.g. 'In the end you need a friend')				
5 Apply spelling rules (e.g. 'i' before 'e' except after 'c' when the sound is 'ee' as in meet)				
6 Use spelling patterns (e.g. fright, slight, night, bright, etc.)				
7 Words in the same family (e.g. refer, referee, reference)				

Introduction as a class

Compare and contrast the ways in which Daniel Defoe and Bill Bryson have selected to introduce their travel writing about Britain and describe Liverpool.

You have already done the basic preparation for writing this essay in the previous lesson. Your comparison grid provides you not only with the structure and key content of your essay but the textual evidence to support your points. This evidence will be needed in the main body of your essay to support the points that you are making. As you know, you need to 'flex your PECs':

- Make a **P**oint
- Use brief quotation from the text as **E**vidence to support your point
- **C**omment on the significance of some of the quotations.

Constructing sentences that do this coherently can be difficult. To help you, your teacher is going to show you how to construct effective sentences about the tone of the two writers.

Working a quotation into a sentence can cause problems as the grammar of the quotation may not fit well with the grammar of your sentence. You may have to redraft your sentence to accommodate the quotation.

Listen and watch carefully as your teacher demonstrates how to do this (**Worksheet 28**). Then, using your whiteboards or a piece of paper, see if you can come up with good ways of expressing the two points, supporting them with evidence and commenting on their significance, using some of the suggestions on page 35.

Sentence starter introducing point	Linking phrase	Supporting evidence	Comment on significance
1 Bryson's witty tone and irony	can be illustrated by	They were having a festival of litter when I arrived	This is effective because …
	is exemplified by		This is entertaining because …
2 Defoe's serious purpose	is summed up by	here is the present state of the country described	Such a statement makes it clear that …
	can be seen in		This immediately makes the reader think that …

Furthermore, commenting on a writer's style often requires integrating a series of short quotations into one sentence which can make drafting effective sentences tricky. And, of course, you have to remember to put quotation marks around any text that has been quoted. The example below reminds you how to do this.

> Bryson's use of description like 'fluttered gaily' and 'brought colour and texture', which would normally be used to describe a thing of beauty, drives home the irony of the passage.

Development *on your own*

Think about the ingredients of effective introduction writing and how this essay could begin. You have around 30 minutes to concentrate on writing your essay. Five minutes before the end of your allocated time, your teacher will remind you to read through your work carefully, correcting any errors of expression, punctuation or spelling and indicating any significant redrafting that may be necessary.

Plenary

Read your partner's essay and see if you agree with their suggestions for improving their work. Discuss the best way forward for each essay and note down the key improvements you've agreed on. Remember:

- Is the essay clearly introduced in a way that makes you feel interested in reading on?
- Have all the key points been covered – purpose, theme, style – and supported by appropriate quotation from the text?

homework

Complete the final draft of your essay, checking that you have answered the question coherently.

> **!** **Remember** to read through your work again carefully, correcting any errors of expression, punctuation or spelling, and write a brief comment on how well you think you have completed the task.

Aims

On these two pages you will:

● Explore how travel writing can convey information and thoughts in an entertaining way.

● Use vivid descriptive detail including figurative imagery and the rhythm and sound of language to make your travel writing come alive.

Starter

As you have discovered, travel writing not only often recounts an engaging story but also provides much information, entertainment and inspiring description. Like all writing, the content very much relies on the purpose of the writer – some travel writers throw more light upon themselves than on the surroundings that supposedly inspired the writing.

Today you are going to be a travel writer yourself. First, list five or so different places that you have been to that have made a strong impression on you in some way – perhaps because they were very beautiful or ugly, or because something very funny or frightening happened while you were there. The places could be very near to where you live now or a very long way away – anywhere in the world. Now select the most promising of your choices and use **Worksheet 29** to help you brainstorm the association of ideas you have with your chosen location, as in the example on the right. Remember to choose somewhere that you can write about entertainingly as well as informatively, including vivid description and imagery as well as making use of the sound effects of language appropriately.

Vivid memory for descriptive passage
15th & final day of amazing festival involving all inhabitants – most colourful costumes ever seen – women wearing layer after layer (over 50) of multi-coloured skirts – only our boatload of 16 tourists – beautiful location.

Location:
Tequile Island
(Lake Titicaca, Peru)

Information to be included
Co-operative society – no interest in developing tourism – control entry to island to defend lifestyle.
Lake Titicaca – highest navigable lake in world.
Over 70 miles long and 40 miles wide.
Altitude 12,000' Depth over 1000'.

Entertaining incident or reflection
Only one colour film – no film for sale – only one shop which sold essentials.
One old woman got annoyed with all the skirts and started removing them – seemed happier once taken off about 50 – still seemed to have around 50 left.
All islanders drunk – no sailor sober enough next day to steer boat many miles to mainland.

Introduction as a class

Now consider purpose, audience and structure so that you can plan your writing effectively.

● *Purpose* To write an entertaining, informative, colourful account of a place you have visited that both amuses the reader and enables them to picture the scene vividly.

● *Audience* Other teenagers of your own age.

- *Structure* Should it be chronological like Mark Twain's or Dervla Murphy's travel writing? Or idiosyncratic – reflecting the highly personal thought patterns that flashed through the mind of the writer – like Bill Bryson, who follows one diverting thought after another before returning to the storyline?

Your planning in the starter activity has narrowed down the location and related themes and incidents that you will be describing. So now you need to consider style. Look at the panel below.

Style

1 *Imagery*

What areas are you going to focus on to describe vividly? What images will you include, for example:

- Similes
- Metaphors
- Personification?

2 *The sound of language*

What sound effects are you going to use, for example:

- Alliteration
- Assonance
- Onomatopoeia
- Repetition
- Rhythm?

3 *Tone*

Given the range of purpose that you have here, a range of tone will be necessary. You will need to decide how you are going to make aspects of your writing humorous.

Development *on your own*

Now it's time to begin. Decide how you are going to make your opening paragraph engage your audience. Remember to select your words and phrases carefully to evoke exactly the tone, mood and image that you are trying to recreate.

Plenary

Listen carefully to some of the extracts that are read out. Discuss what makes them effective. Think about how the extracts are entertaining, and informative as well as evocative.

Reflect on what you have written so far:

- Have you communicated your ideas coherently?
- Do sections of your writing vividly recreate the scene so that the reader can picture it?
- Are sections of your writing entertaining?
- Have you used the power of words effectively to evoke images and sound effects?
- Have you effectively conveyed some information about the place/event described?

Jot down any points that you think need strengthening.

homework

Redraft your work in the light of your comments.

> **!** **Remember** to improve your work in the light of the above points and write a brief comment on how well you have completed the task. Make sure all the words are spelt correctly. Add any words you had difficulty with to your spelling log.

Reviewing what's been learnt

In this section you have read and discussed stories from other cultures, thought about different ways of structuring narrative and what difference an author's perspective makes to the meaning of text. You have also put yourself in the shoes of an outsider and experimented with ways of structuring your story to make it more effective.

You have looked at how the English language has incorporated words from other cultures and seen how specialist dictionaries can be used to help you understand specialized vocabulary. You have analysed what words cause you spelling problems and decided the best route to rectify this.

You have also discussed the creative and entertaining features of travel writing and compared travel writing from different times as well as trying to make your own travel writing entertaining, informative and evocative.

Much of the work in this section has focused on discussing the effectiveness of different ways of writing. Consider what contribution you made to that discussion, identifying your strengths as well as areas that need improving. You started off the year reflecting on your reading, writing, and speaking and listening targets. In this section you've also determined your spelling targets. Now it's time to reconsider those targets in the light of what you have achieved in this section and set yourself new targets.

The aspects of my English that I have improved in this section are:
-
-
-
-
-

My targets for the next section are:
-
-
-
-
-

Inform, explain, describe

Introduction

In the first part of this section you will be studying some key features and scenes from Shakespeare's tragedy *Macbeth*. You will consider the ways in which the playwright engages the interest and attention of the audience through imagery and the way the characters interact with each other. You will begin to understand why Shakespeare is still the most popular and well-known dramatist in the world today.

Shakespeare would have written all his plays by hand – in his day a printing press was a relatively recent invention. Four hundred years later, we have computers which not only process our words for us, but find information, send messages and store files. Almost everything we need is literally at the tips of our fingers – information can be accessed and transferred instantaneously.

In the second part of this section you will consider how ICT can help us to access and process information, as well as enable us to communicate with the rest of the world. You will be looking at ways to search for and select information, and to create a website of your own on a given topic.

Key aims

In this section you will:

- Analyse the language, form and dramatic impact of a Shakespearean play.
- Research and integrate information using a range of sources, with an ICT focus, so that you can shape material to meet your readers' needs.

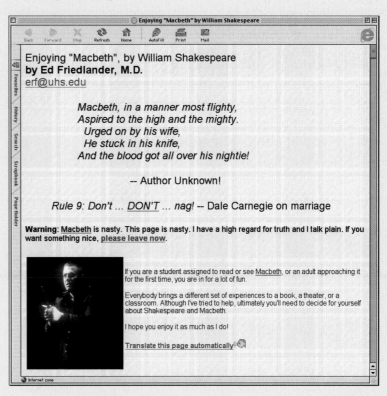

The tragedy of Macbeth

Aims

On these two pages you will:
- Be introduced to the story of Shakespeare's play *Macbeth*.
- Gain an understanding as to why this play is still popular.
- Test your knowledge of the story of the play.

Starter *as a group*

You have been asked to make a film that will attract a large audience and hopefully become a box office hit for years to come. Working in groups of four, decide what ingredients you will choose for your film. You have only four minutes to discuss your plans.

Briefly describe the kind of setting, characters, plot and themes. Be prepared to give feedback to the class, but this should take no longer than one minute for each group.

Introduction *as a class*

Today you will be exploring the story of one of Shakespeare's most popular plays, *Macbeth*. For some of you, this play will also be the examination text for your National Curriculum Test in May. For the first time you will be taking a literature test on a set text that you have previously studied in class. However, this is not the only reason for studying *Macbeth*.

Over the centuries, many millions of people have enjoyed performances of this spellbinding play. The fact that *Macbeth* contains murders, witchcraft, blood and gore, supernatural forces, a struggle between good and evil, strong characters and, incidentally,

that it is the shortest of Shakespeare's plays, may have something to do with the fact that it is still one of his most popular plays!

Macbeth is the story of a good man drawn into evil by dark forces and the temptation of witchcraft. He becomes ambitious, craving power and murdering the king so as to become king himself. He then begins a reign of terror over his people but never feels secure or free from guilt. What is tragic about Macbeth is not so much that he did terrible deeds, but that he only realized the wrong he had done just as he died – too late to put things right and redeem his soul.

Your teacher will show you a video of *Macbeth*. As you watch the video, think about the discussion points on page 41. At the end of each Act, your teacher will stop the video. Be prepared to contribute to a class discussion on the questions.

Responding to a performance of *Macbeth*

Act 1: up to the point where Macbeth and his wife have plotted the murder of King Duncan.

1 How has Shakespeare used the supernatural in Act 1 to engage the interest of the audience?

2 Describe Macbeth's character in a few words. Cover both his good and bad points.

3 What impression does Lady Macbeth create in your mind? Does she also have good and bad characteristics?

Act 2: up to the point where Duncan's murder has been discovered and Macbeth plays the innocent.

4 In what ways do Macbeth and his wife react differently after the king has been murdered?

5 Do you think anyone suspects that they are guilty when Duncan has been found?

6 How has Shakespeare kept the audience interested in Act 2?

Act 3: up to the point where the Lords of Scotland are suspicious following Macbeth's banquet and Banquo's murder.

7 Do you think Macbeth needed to murder his friend Banquo? Why do you think he did it?

8 What effect does the appearance of Banquo's ghost have on Macbeth, and on the audience? What theme does this relate to?

9 What is your opinion of Macbeth at this point in the play?

Acts 4 and 5: to the end of the play.

10 Why do you think Shakespeare made Macbeth go back to the witches?

11 How does this scene interest the audience?

12 By the end of the play, how do we know that the witches have tricked Macbeth?

General comments about the play as a whole.

13 What did you most enjoy?

Development *as a group*

Before studying the playscript, it is important to make sure you have a good knowledge of the story as a whole. Then you will be better able to concentrate on the characters and language and the way the themes develop.

In groups of four, and using the information you have gained from the video, sort out the cards your teacher will give you (**Worksheet 30**) into the correct chronological sequence to tell the story of *Macbeth*.

Feed back to the class and see whether you all agree on the correct order of events.

Plenary

Think back to the starter activity where you were planning to make a box office hit movie. How many of the ingredients you chose are present in *Macbeth*?

Macbeth and history

Aims

On these two pages you will:

- Examine the historical context of *Macbeth*.
- Explain why Shakespeare changed historical details for his own dramatic purposes.
- Investigate how English has changed over time.

Starter *as a group*

Shakespeare's language is different from the English we use today. Nearly 400 years have passed since he wrote his plays, and the English language has continued to evolve.

The first printing press

The printing press was invented in Germany about 1440 and introduced into England by William Caxton in 1476. Standardization of the language gradually followed, as printers tried to ensure that words were spelt the same way.

For example, in Shakespearean times, people used the forms 'thee' and 'thou' to address each other. While this usage may have survived in areas of northern England, elsewhere it has died out and now we simply use the word 'you'. The invention of the printing press in the 15th century led to the gradual standardization of vocabulary, grammar and spelling. Many verbs were made to conform to regular patterns.

As English changes, some words fall out of use altogether, sometimes the way a word is spelt may change, or a word may come to mean something else.

Your teacher will give you copies of **Worksheet 31**. Working in groups of four, discuss and answer the questions. Be prepared to feed back to the class.

Introduction *as a group*

Shakespeare wrote *Macbeth* in 1606. The play retells the story of Macbeth, King of Scotland from 1040 to 1057. Shakespeare wrote not only for the enjoyment of the wider public but also for political reasons; he was especially anxious to flatter and entertain his new king, James I of England (James VI of Scotland).

Two themes of the play – the nature of kingship and the supernatural – addressed particular concerns of Shakespeare's audience:

- It was important to have a trustworthy king. James was a descendant of the real, historical Banquo. In *Macbeth*, Shakespeare turns Banquo into one of the good characters.

King James VI of Scotland and James I of England

- James and his subjects fully believed witchcraft to be a real and dangerous influence in their world.

- In those days, people believed that the king was God's appointed leader on Earth and what he did was of great significance. To rebel against the king was equivalent to overturning the accepted order of things.

Working in groups of four, think back to the story of the play that you studied in the previous lesson. Discuss the ways in which Macbeth shows himself to be a bad king (e.g. 'He is suspicious of everyone around him'). Then, from this discussion, draw up a list of the opposites which would be the criteria for a good king (e.g. 'A king needs to trust his people').

Be prepared to feed back to the class.

Development as a group

To appreciate the political and historical context of *Macbeth*, it is also helpful to understand how Shakespeare changed the historical account of Scotland's King Macbeth to suit his purposes. He was very selective in the 'facts' that he used for his play.

The reality was very different from the drama. The real King Macbeth appears to have ruled Scotland well and to have given the country a period of stability. Shakespeare, however, created a villainous man who would stop at nothing to achieve and secure power. This complete reversal of the facts indicates that Shakespeare must have had broader intentions when he wrote the play.

Working in groups of four, examine the historical account of King Macbeth on **Worksheet 32** and compare it with the story of the play that you worked on in the last lesson.

1 Add the details about Shakespeare's version in the second column on the worksheet.

2 In the third column, say why you think Shakespeare changed the facts, for example to create tension, flatter his king, to be politically correct, to add suspense, etc.

Be prepared to feed back to the class.

Plenary

Give three reasons why Shakespeare changed the historical facts in his play *Macbeth*.

Shakespeare's imagery

Aims

On these two pages you will:

- Understand how Shakespeare created a dramatic impact through his descriptive imagery.
- Describe the effect of horror and fear created by Macbeth's words in Act 1 scene 2.
- Write a parody of the witches in Act 1 scene 1 of *Macbeth*.

Starter in pairs

Sometimes writers imitate other writers' work by exaggerating the stylistic features, and often the content, of the original for humorous effect. Works that mimic others in this way are called **parodies**. Ever since Shakespeare created the witches in the opening scene of *Macbeth*, other people have stolen his idea and mimicked it in the form of parody.

Today you will be writing your own parody of the opening scene. Imagine a 21st-century version of the play: in the opening scene the witches may not be on the heath, out in the cold and the rain, but in their electronic caves sending e-mails to each other. What would they say?

Working in pairs, use **Worksheets 33a–b** to parody Shakespeare's words by turning them into e-mail messages. To be true to the spirit of parody you shouldn't change the essential nature of what the witches are saying.

> **parody** a composition which mimics the style of another author in a humorous way

Introduction as a class

In Shakespeare's day there were no special effects which would create a supernatural atmosphere of fear and horror on stage and entertain the audience. Plays were performed in daylight and, as Shakespeare could not use projected images or special lighting, he used other devices. He created scenery and illusions with the power of his words and the actors' skilful performances.

In Act 2 scene 1 Macbeth is about to murder King Duncan, as he and his wife have planned. To Shakespeare's audience this would have been a terrible crime, as the king was believed to be God's representative on Earth. Macbeth does not undertake the deed lightly. As he approaches the chamber, he is filled with guilt and fear. Suddenly a ghostly dagger appears which seems to point the way to Duncan.

Listen to the reading of the speech on **Worksheet 34**. When Macbeth delivers this speech, he is alone on stage. A **soliloquy** such as this is often used to tell us what a character is really thinking; we learn a great deal about what is going on in Macbeth's mind concerning the murder he is about to commit. The sudden appearance of the imaginary dagger floating in the air is used to create an atmosphere of fear and horror. In order for the illusion to be effective, the audience has to believe in it as much as Macbeth does.

> **soliloquy** a speech in a play when a character is alone and speaks their thoughts aloud

In pairs, examine the way in which Shakespeare helps the audience to see the dagger that Macbeth sees in front of him (lines 33–49).

- What does it look like?
- What does it do?
- How does Macbeth react to it?
- What does this tell you about Macbeth's state of mind?

Now use your answers to these questions to help you perform lines 33–49 of the speech. One person should read the lines, while the other plays the part of Macbeth, putting actions to the words. Explain what you have learned and describe what you experienced to the class.

Development ・in pairs

In the second part of the speech (lines 49–64), Macbeth's words create a dark vision of death and horror. The images, symbolizing evil, prepare the audience for the foul deed that is about to occur.

1 In pairs, highlight on your photocopy of the speech those words and phrases which create an atmosphere of evil through references to the supernatural, death and blood. Use a different colour for each if you like.

2 Describe the images that these words create in your mind. What do they make you think about?

3 Explain what these words tell us about Macbeth's state of mind at the time.

When you give your feedback, mention how and why Shakespeare has placed so much emphasis on the evil and horror of the act Macbeth was about to perform.

Plenary

Identify three devices that Shakespeare uses to engage the interest of his audience in Act 2 scene 1.

homework

Answer this question for homework: 'What is the dramatic impact of Macbeth's soliloquy in Act 2 scene 1? How does Shakespeare engage the interest of the audience?'

Use the information that you have gathered during the lesson to guide your response.

> **!** **Remember** when writing always:
> Check – revise – correct – refine, before you write your final presentation piece.
> - Distinguish the play, *Macbeth*, from the character Macbeth by using either italics or inverted commas.

Interpreting a scene

Aims

On these two pages you will:

- Analyse the way in which the language of the play creates atmosphere.
- Develop and compare different interpretations of *Macbeth* Act 2 scene 2.
- Understand how different interpretations in performance influence our perception of characters in a play.

> *Enter Macbeth*
> LADY MACBETH   My husband
> MACBETH   I have done the deed. Didst thou not hear a noise?
> LADY MACBETH   I heard the owl scream and the crickets cry. Did not you speak?
> MACBETH   When?
> LADY MACBETH   Now.
> MACBETH   As I descended?
> LADY MACBETH   Ay.
> MACBETH   Hark!
>   Who lies i' th' second chamber?
> LADY MACBETH   Donalbain.
> *Looking on his hands*
> MACBETH   This is a sorry sight.
> LADY MACBETH   A foolish thought to say a sorry sight.

Starter *in pairs*

Directors and actors of plays have to decide how to create a particular mood or atmosphere. Depending on how the words are spoken – the expression and pace – the audience may interpret the same scene very differently. You are going to explore what effect expression has by doing the following activity.

Read the dialogue from the beginning of *Macbeth* Act 2 scene 2 (above right). Your teacher will give you a card which will brief you to say the words with a particular tone and expression (**Worksheet 35**). Practise delivering the lines in the mood or tone suggested on your card. It is important to keep the instructions on your card a secret from other pairs.

In your pairs, be prepared to read your dialogue to the class.

1 As you listen to others, try to guess which effect they were directed to create.

2 Discuss which interpretation you think created the most effective atmosphere.

3 Which interpretation do you think Shakespeare intended?

Introduction *as a class*

Today you are going to look at how Shakespeare develops an atmosphere or mood between the two central characters in *Macbeth*. We do not see the murder of Duncan on the stage. Instead, Shakespeare concentrates our attention on the dramatic aftermath and the effect it has on Macbeth and Lady Macbeth.

The contrasting way in which these two people react to the successful outcome of their plot to murder Duncan tells us a great deal about the characters. The loud knocking at the gate at the end of the scene increases the suspense as we wonder whether they will be caught.

Read the extract from *Macbeth* Act 2 scene 2, lines 30–74, on **Worksheet 36**.

on your own

At the end of this activity you will join forces with your partner, but to start with, you will be working on your own. Partner A should focus on Macbeth's words and consider the following questions:

1 What do you learn about Macbeth's state of mind and feelings following the murder of Duncan?

2 What are all the things Macbeth has suddenly come to fear?

3 What atmosphere does Shakespeare create through Macbeth's words?

4 How do you think Macbeth should say each of his lines?

Partner B should focus on Lady Macbeth's words and consider the following questions:

1 How does she respond to Macbeth on his return from the murder of Duncan? For example, does she tease him like a drunken lover, or is she like a commander in charge of her troops?

2 Pick out some examples of things that she says. What do they tell you about her character?

3 How do you think Lady Macbeth should say each of her lines?

in pairs

Your teacher will tell you when to join up with your partner so that you can discuss what you have each discovered about your particular character.

Development *as a group*

You have seen how Shakespeare's words can be interpreted in many ways. Depending on how they are given expression on stage, the same words can create a variety of different moods and relationships between the characters. Each new production of a Shakespeare play can lead us to see it and its characters in a different light. One of the reasons for Shakespeare's appeal is this potential to develop alternative viewpoints.

Your teacher will ask you to join up with another pair. Compare your conclusions about Macbeth and Lady Macbeth with theirs. To what extent are your views similar or different?

In your groups of four, imagine you were directing this scene. Decide how you would ask the actors to bring out the mood, tone and atmosphere between Lady Macbeth and her husband at this significant point.

Choose two from your group to become actors, one to be the director and one to be a critical member of the audience. Then act out a short section of about 20 lines, putting your ideas into practice and refining them as appropriate. You may like to annotate the copy of the extract on **Worksheet 36** with actors' or director's notes to help you.

Be ready to perform your piece to the class and give feedback on other performances.

Plenary

What have you learned about the relationship between a playwright's words and the influence of a director? How can a director control the way in which the audience interprets a scene or understands how characters are feeling and responding to situations?

Shakespeare in performance

Aims

On these two pages you will:

- Explain how Shakespeare uses words and actions to create a dramatic effect in Act 3 scene 4.
- Develop different approaches to the production of Act 3 scene 4.
- Write an eyewitness account based on this scene.
- Investigate the impact that Shakespeare has had on the English language.

Starter as a group

Eurosceptic … nimby … spin doctor … website … Have you ever wondered how new words enter into everyday usage?

Read the information about Shakespeare and his influence on the English language on **Worksheet 37**. Talk about any of the points which interest you. Through discussion, try to answer these questions:

1   Why do you think Shakespeare's inventions are still used today?

2   Why do you think there has been a sudden influx of new words into the English language in the last 20 years?

Be prepared to feed back to the class.

Introduction as a class

So far in this section you have studied a soliloquy and a dialogue between Macbeth and his wife. Today you will be looking at the interaction between several characters in Act 3 scene 4. Read the extract from *Macbeth* Act 3 scene 4, lines 46–122, on **Worksheets 38a–b**.

as a group

Each group will be given a different character to study.

1   Discuss the questions (below) associated with your given character.

2   When your teacher tells you, new groups will be formed. Each person will join a group of four as the 'expert' on the character they discussed in task 1. There should be one representative in each group of the four characters so everyone will have feedback from each of the discussions.

Macbeth
Examine Macbeth's words and actions in this extract. Explain what you think his mood and state of mind are at this point in the play. Select different points in the text and explain what he is thinking and why he behaves as he does.

Lady Macbeth
Examine Lady Macbeth's words and actions in this extract. Explain how she responds to the situation and why. What does she think of her husband's odd behaviour? What is her main concern?

Lords of Scotland, e.g. Lennox and Ross
Examine the way in which the Lords respond to what is happening. Explain what you think their thoughts might be as they witness Macbeth's strange behaviour. Are they sympathetic or suspicious at the end of the extract when they leave?

Banquo's ghost
Examine the way in which Banquo's ghost appears and disappears. How does the appearance of the ghost affect Macbeth? Explain why you think Shakespeare has included his ghost at this point in the play. What effect does it have on the audience?

Development *as a group*

A Shakespeare play was intended to be experienced by an audience as a performance on stage, rather than to be studied in a classroom. A director has the task of revealing to the audience, as far as possible, the full effect of Shakespeare's intentions. The play *Macbeth* is full of scenes which present a challenge to a director.

Imagine that you are producing a performance of *Macbeth* on stage.

1   Each group will be given a different aspect of the production of Act 3 scene 4 to consider (below).

2   Discuss your options and agree your group's approach.

3   Feed back to the class, using visual aids if appropriate.

Plenary

What do you consider to be the main problems in trying to produce this scene on stage?

homework

Imagine you are Ross or Lennox, and write an eyewitness account of events at the banquet. Include some direct quotations and conclude with a few personal comments concerning King Macbeth's rather odd behaviour.

> **!** **Remember** When writing always: Check – revise – correct – refine, before you write your final presentation piece.
> • Make effective use of descriptive detail.

aside words spoken in an undertone on stage which other actors are not supposed to hear

Banquo's ghost

If you were producing *Macbeth*, describe what you would do to create the effect of Banquo's ghost. For example, would you have the actor playing Banquo actually appear, would you project an image or have nothing at all and let the audience imagine the ghost through Macbeth's actions alone?

Costumes

Describe the costumes that each of the main actors – Macbeth, Lady Macbeth, Ross and Lennox – would wear. Think about colours and texture as well as style. Would the costumes be similar to one another or contrasting to show different status? Would they be in modern day dress or from another era?

Stage and props

If you were producing Act 3 scene 4, describe how you would set up the stage. Draw a plan of the stage, indicating where the actors would come and go and where they would be at the beginning, middle and end of the scene. List the props you would need.

Director's notes

As the director of the play, annotate the script on **Worksheets 38a–b** to show how you would like the actors to say their lines, for example fearfully, whispering, angrily, with authority, etc. Make it clear that some lines are being spoken as **asides**, privately between Macbeth and his wife, while other lines are addressed to the assembled group as a whole.

49

Writing about Shakespeare

Aims

On these two pages you will:

- Hotseat some of Shakespeare's characters.
- Review what you have learnt so far about how Shakespeare entertains his audience.
- Write a formal essay using diverse information and showing clear links between points, evidence and commentary.

Starter  on your own

Imagine that, at the end of *Macbeth* Act 3 scene 4, you were able to meet the following characters:

- Macbeth
- Lady Macbeth
- Banquo's ghost
- Lennox.

Think of three questions that you would like to ask each of them. You could ask about how they feel, what they are thinking or for an explanation for their actions so far in the play.

 as a class

Your teacher and chosen members of the class will undertake to act in role as these characters from *Macbeth*. While they are in the 'hotseat', the rest of the class will ask the characters the questions they have already prepared.

Introduction on your own

You have studied three important scenes in *Macbeth*: Act 2 scenes 1 and 2, and Act 3 scene 4. Now you are going to write an essay which will draw together the points you have learnt about the play.

The title for your essay is:

> Explain how Shakespeare interests and entertains audiences with reference to the three key scenes you have studied in *Macbeth*:
> - **Act 2 scenes 1 and 2**
> - **Act 3 scene 4.**

To write a successful response to the essay you will need to begin by brainstorming what things were interesting and entertaining in these scenes. Think about all the work you have done on the scenes so far. Use **Worksheet 39** to help you gather evidence for your essay, organizing your thoughts under these headings:

- Purpose and plot
- Scenes and topics
- Character
- Language and imagery
- Dramatic technique.

Your teacher will give you a time limit for your research, so use your time effectively and be ready to give feedback to the class when your time is up.

Development on your own

Once you have gathered your evidence, you need to plan what you are going to say and the order in which you will make your points. The flowchart on page 51 may help you structure your essay. Then refer to **Worksheet 40** to help you plan and organize your essay.

Introduction

The introduction needs to:

- Show that you have understood the question
- Provide an outline of your views.

↓

Development

In this section, you can begin to develop your answer to the question.

- Choose the three points which made the greatest impression on you.
- Cover each of your points in turn, beginning with the most important.
- Write a paragraph on each point.
- Select the best examples to support the points you are making.
- Try and link your paragraphs, so that your argument flows logically.

↓

Conclusion

At the end of your essay you need to:

- Draw together the main threads of your argument
- Summarize your main points
- Give an indication of your personal opinion where appropriate
- Conclude by giving your answer to the essay question.

Flex your PECs: Point – Evidence – Comment

- Begin by making a **Point**, e.g.:
  'The introduction of the supernatural in Act 2 scene 1, where Macbeth sees the "air-drawn dagger" leading him to Duncan's chamber, would capture the interest of the audience …'
- Back it up with **Evidence** quoted from the text, e.g.:
  'Come, let me clutch thee.
  I have thee not, and yet I see thee still.'
- Finally make a **Comment** about the quotation relating it to your main point, e.g.:
  'Remembering the witches, the audience would be seized by the idea that Macbeth is somehow being controlled by a force that is beyond his power, in this case a dagger that can be seen but not touched.'

Plenary

Why do people still go to watch *Macbeth*, a play written 400 years ago?

homework

Write the essay that you have been planning in this lesson.

> **!** **Remember** When writing always: Check – revise – correct – refine, before you write your final presentation piece.
> - Quotations are essential: they show you have a good knowledge and understanding of the text. Keep them brief, never more than four lines, and to the point. Use inverted commas to show when you have used quotations and, if there are two lines or more, put them on separate lines using the same format as in the play.
> - Refer to the 'play' not the 'book' and the 'audience' not the 'reader'.
> - Keep your expression and tone formal at all times.

At home on the web

Aims

On these two pages you will:

- Discuss the features of a website home page.
- Evaluate the design of a particular home page.
- Choose a topic for the creation of a group website.
- Review the advantages and disadvantages of different forms of information text.
- Investigate the way word meanings have changed over time.

Starter *in pairs*

Words are always changing and evolving to suit the needs of the people who use them. Today you are going to look at some modern words which have recently developed dual meanings as they have become linked with the world of ICT and the Internet.

Give the ordinary everyday meaning of these words and the meaning they have taken on as ICT terms:

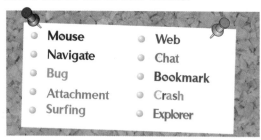

Mouse	Web
Navigate	Chat
Bug	Bookmark
Attachment	Crash
Surfing	Explorer

How and why do you think these words have come to have their new meanings? What is the link between the everyday meaning of each word and its new ICT meaning? How many other words can you think of that have similarly developed dual meanings linked with ICT? Give your feedback to the class.

Introduction *as a group*

Interactive technology such as the Internet should be designed to respond to, and support the needs of, the user. A well-constructed website will be easy to understand and **navigate** to find information. The home page usually gives a good indication of how helpful the site as a whole might be.

The home page is the name given to the first page of a website. It acts like the contents page of a book, or the introductory first screen of a CD-ROM. Unlike a book, however, clicking on buttons or underlined words on the screen will take you directly to the information you have requested. These are called **hot links**. You can navigate your way around the site using these hot links, clicking on buttons that are often grouped together in navigation bars. Good sites always have a way of returning to the home page by having a hot link at the bottom of every page, so that you don't get lost.

Examine the home page for the USA Environmental Protection Agency (EPA) on page 53.

1 Discuss the form and purpose of all the features that are labelled.

2 Assess how easy you think you would find this website to use. Refer to the questions on **Worksheet 41** to focus your thoughts.

---

hot link a word or phrase that can be selected to link users to another part of the website, or to a different website
navigate to find your way around a text

3 Use your responses to the questions on **Worksheet 41** to draw up a checklist of points that you think are important considerations when creating a good home page for a website.

Development as a group

There are many organizations like EPA which provide information on subjects of global concern. Your teacher will give you a copy of **Worksheet 42** which tells you about your World at Risk Website Challenge. Your group will respond to the challenge, research a topic and create a website.

Brainstorm your ideas and discuss the questions on the worksheet. Assign each member of the group a specific area to research, making sure that you divide up the investigation work fairly. Your teacher will provide you with areas to research if you need help.

Plenary

On your whiteboards or paper, write down three things that you think are the top considerations when creating a good home page for a website.

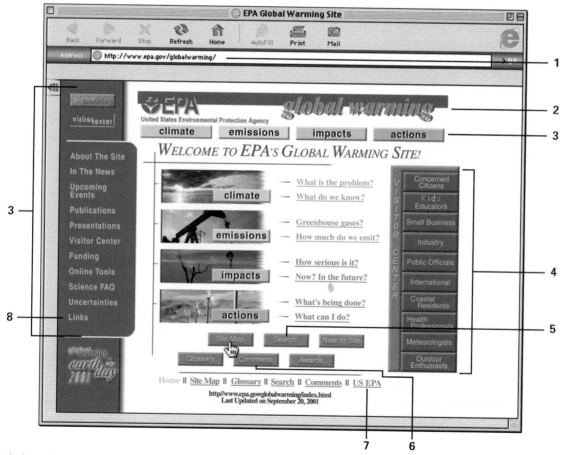

1 website address
2 website logo
3 fixed navigation bars that stay on screen as you move from page to page

4 navigation bar to let you select your route
5 search button to let you search site for information
6 comments button to let you e-mail questions and comments

7 navigation bar that ends each page of the site
8 button that links to other relevant sites

Selecting and weighing up

Aims

On these two pages you will:

- Evaluate the reliability of information sources.
- Review research strategies.
- Practise research skills independently for your group website.

Starter

In the last lesson you were asked to choose a topic for your group's response to the World at Risk Website Challenge. Today you will look at strategies that could be used to evaluate and select the information you need.

1 Consider whether all the information that is available in print and on the Internet is equally reliable. Consider the way in which books, magazines and newspapers are published. They involve a process in which writers, editors and publishers take responsibility for the information they publish. Sources are quoted, checked and acknowledged. How far is this also true of information on the Internet? Once an organization or an individual has purchased the web space, they can, in theory, put whatever they like onto their site. How can you tell whether or not it is reliable?

2 Draw up a list of questions that you think would be useful to test the reliability of a website that you have found. For example, 'Is this site run by a special interest group who may be biased?' 'When was it written?'

Each group should be prepared to give feedback to the class.

Introduction as a class

Once you have the source that you want in front of you, and you are happy that it is reliable, it is time to select the precise information from it that you need. Study this flowchart as a class:

Begin by knowing exactly what it is that you need to find out: set yourself some questions on the topic that you need to answer.

Scan the article, looking for some key words linked with your topic.

If using a photocopy or printout, highlight areas of the text where you think your answers might be.

Look again at the highlighted areas, read the information there more closely and make sure that it answers your question.

Think about what you have read and look away from the extract, then write the answer to the question in your own words.

If necessary go back to the passage to select a short quotation to support what you have written, but do this only if you think the quotation will really add something to your response.

as a group

Use this method to research some specific questions on global warming, using a newspaper article by Paul Brown as your source. In groups of five:

1 Read the article on global warming carefully (**Worksheet 43**).

2 Look at the five questions that you need to answer in the box on the right. Each member of the group should select one question to be the focus of their research.

3 Follow the steps in the flowchart on page 54 to select the information that you need.

4 Report back to your group with the answer to your question.

Feed back to the class and compare answers to each of the questions. If they are too similar to one another, it probably means that you have kept too close to the text and not used enough of your own words.

When the ice caps melt through global warming, the sea level rises

Questions for Research on Global Warming Topic

1 What scientific evidence is there that the world is getting hotter?

2 How has the dangerous effect of global warming increased in the last ten years?

3 What are companies/industries doing to lessen the effects of pollution?

4 What other signs or effects of global warming can we expect in the future?

5 Is the world doing enough to prevent the serious effects of global warming?

Development *as a group*

In your groups come up with five different questions that you think will help you search for the information you will need to create your web pages for the Website Challenge. Each member of the group should then choose a question for their homework research.

If you cannot find the answers to your questions, consider these possibilities:

● Are you asking the right question?

● Do you need to continue with your research?

Plenary

What reasons would you give for saying that Paul Brown's article on global warming was reliable? What reservations might you have about its reliability?

How do you extract the information that you need from a source? Write three tips on your whiteboards.

homework

Undertake the research necessary to answer the question that you have agreed with the rest of your team. Complete this and bring the results to the next lesson, remembering to use what you have learnt in the lesson about effective strategies for finding useful information.

How websites are structured

Aims

On these two pages you will:

- Understand how web pages are linked with one another.
- Examine a website map and begin to design your own website, choosing a range of presentational devices.
- Analyse how media texts influence and are influenced by readers.

Starter *as a group*

Media texts aim to influence readers, but they are also influenced by readers. For example, daily newspapers rely more and more on pictures because readers are used to getting their news from the television and expect it to be visual.

Look again at the home page of the EPA global warming website on page 53 (if possible, access the site on screen) and discuss the following:

1 Look at the way the centre of the home page is designed. How does this attempt to influence visitors to the site?

2 Look at the design of the whole home page. Find at least three pieces of evidence to show that the needs of visitors have influenced the design of this site.

3 If you are online, look at the 'Kids' website. Identify three key differences between the 'Kids' site and the others and explain why you think these differences exist.

Be prepared to feed your ideas back to the class.

Introduction *as a group*

When you use a reference book you can see at a glance the way in which the book is made up of chapters and/or sections and the order in which they follow one another. There will be contents and index pages to guide you, and when there are several references that you need to look up, you may use pieces of paper as markers to help you find your place again quickly.

Websites too have pages. The difference is that web pages are interactive, sometimes they also have moving images, and they are linked with one another electronically. The buttons or hot links may give you access to different parts of the site, or link you to different websites.

In groups, examine the site map on **Worksheet 44**. This is a map of the EPA site, whose home page you studied earlier.

Discuss:

- How does the design of the site as a whole take the needs of the visitor into consideration?
- What additional support has been provided for visitors to the site to understand and explore the information that is being provided by the site?
- Why is it important for visitors to be able to interact directly with the information on the page?

Be prepared to feed back to the class.

Development *as a group*

Once you have understood something about how websites are constructed, you can begin to structure your own. As a first step, your website should have a home page and five information pages linked to it – one for each member of the group. As you start to build your website, you may need to consider having extra pages in order to cover all your material and to prevent the pages becoming too cluttered.

In your groups:

1   Decide what the linking pages will have as their focus. Each one should answer a different question, based on the areas you have each researched. Perhaps your research has led you to believe that there are more important areas of information that you would like to give your visitors.

2   Create a site map showing how your pages will be linked to the home page and to one another.

3   Decide what special features you want to include, such as a site map or a button for feedback. Are you going to have buttons for these on the home page?

4   Agree on the design so that all the pages have a unified look. Consider the following presentational features:

○   **Name** of your organization and its logo

○   **Overall layout** – use of boxes, bullets, etc.

○   **Art work** – drawings, photographs, clip art

○   **Font** – type styles and sizes that you would like to use

○   **Colour scheme** – this is an important consideration as people are naturally attracted to certain colour combinations

○   **Use of space** – it is important that the page should not be too cluttered.

At this point it is enough to have a draft site map. The final drafts will need to be considered in the next lesson, following the homework research by individuals for the material they need to create their page.

Plenary

Why is it important to have a carefully structured website? Why do people constructing websites have to plan their site together before they begin to make their individual pages?

homework

Complete the research on your given topic and plan a draft outline of your web page.

> **!** **Remember** that it is very important to keep track of your sources so that you can acknowledge them later on.

Creating your own web pages

Aims

On these two pages you will:

- Identify and explore the features that make an effective website.
- Synthesize information from a range of sources, shaping it to suit your purpose and audience.
- Make use of a range of presentational devices.
- Recognize your own strengths and weaknesses as spellers, experimenting with ways to remember problem words.

Starter  on your own

A computer can only recognize exact words, not near misses. Accurate spelling is very important when you are typing in a search word or website address.

To help you improve your spelling:

- Make a list of five words you always seem to have a problem with.
- Check how to spell them by using a dictionary.
- Write the correct spelling alongside your original spelling – how many have you actually got right?
- Think of a way to help you remember the ones you got wrong.

 in pairs

- Test each other on all five words. Have you remembered how to spell them?
- If not, help each other to think of an effective way to remember the correct spelling.

Introduction

Today you will be evaluating the features of a quality website. Then you will construct your own as part of the Website Challenge.

There are four essential points to look for when judging the effectiveness of a website. Remember them as the '4 As':

1 Accessible

Your site has to be user friendly for your intended visitors (11–14-year-olds). This means it must be easy for them to find the information that they need. It also makes reading on screen easier if you have hot links to other parts of your web page. The links and navigation points should be obvious, so no one gets lost.

2 Accurate

It is up to you to make sure that the information you give is accurate and reliable. Quote your sources, so that people can check them for themselves if they wish. To do this, you may want to have links to the websites you used, so quote their web addresses.

3 Appropriate

Make sure that the information you give and the language you use is suitable for your target audience. Don't blind your visitors with scientific words. Where these can't be avoided, make a glossary through a hot link. Ensure that your sentences are to the point, not long and rambling.

4 Appealing

Your site should be attractive to look at: uncluttered, simple, colourful but not hard on the eyes. Graphics and pictures used with care will create an effect and serve your purpose. Remember that all pages should follow the design that you agreed.

as a group

1 Examine the example of a web page from the EPA Kids' site on the greenhouse effect (**Worksheet 45**).

2 Judge it against the '4 As' criteria.

3 Use **Worksheet 46** to guide your assessment.

Give your feedback to the class.

Development on your own

Now each member of the group should create their own individual website pages which will focus on their specialist area or question as previously agreed. These pages will be hot linked to the group's home page, which you will create together in the next lesson.

1 Use your research material to draw out specific information, shaping it to suit your agreed purpose and audience.

2 Draft your written content, integrating the information you have gathered. Remember the importance of clear, appropriate expression, as well as accurate spelling and punctuation.

3 Draft your web page(s) on screen if possible. Content and layout are important at this stage; don't worry too much about graphics, colours and illustrations yet, as these can come later.

as a group

Read through and check the contributions from the other members of your group. Act as critical friends and help each other out:

- **Reflect on style** – does it suit the purpose and the target audience?
- **Verify the facts** – is the information accurate? How do you know?
- **Consider organization** – is the material in the best, most interesting and helpful order?
- **Check spelling** – words that you are good at may be someone else's weakness.
- **Examine punctuation** – make sure that it is correctly used to help the reader make sense of what is being said.
- **Layout and design** – make helpful suggestions.

Plenary

Each group should feed back to the class on the features that they have considered to be of key importance in their web page design.

homework

Using the feedback from the other members of your group, make the necessary changes to your individual web page and design a final copy. You may, if you wish, do your page design on a computer. Now also is the time to add pictures and graphics.

> **!** **Remember** it is essential that you bring all your final drafts to the next lesson. Without your contributions you will be unable to take part in the work and the celebration of your joint achievement.

The Website Challenge

Aims

On these two pages you will:

- Evaluate some website home pages.
- Create your own home page and put your website together.
- Evaluate the websites of other groups.

Starter  as a group

The home page is a very important feature of every website. It is this page that visitors use to judge the site as a whole. If it does not look clear and inviting they may be put off and not visit the rest of the site.

Look at the examples of website home pages on page 61 and **Worksheets 47** and **48**.

1 Can you identify the purpose and audience for each one?

2 How far do they meet the '4 As' criteria? (Accessible, Accurate, Appropriate, Appealing.)

3 Explain which you think is the best and describe the features that make it effective.

Introduction as a group

Every member of the group should by now have completed the final draft of their web pages for the group's site. In this lesson you will put them together and design the home page that will link them all to the website as a whole.

Follow the steps in the flowchart opposite.

Share the work that you have each done on your individual pages. Check that everyone has followed the agreed design.

↓

Talk about and plan the overall design of the home page. How will you signal to visitors that additional information can be found by exploring the site further? What other features will you need to include?

↓

Each member of the group will need to summarize the topic of their own web page in a few words. This will go on the home page, and will draw the visitors to their pages. You will need to agree on the form that each of these summaries will take.

↓

Now create the home page for your website. Make sure that your hot links are clear and that it is easy to access the information to be found on other pages. Put your key buttons into a navigation bar and make sure it stays with you as you move through the site.

↓

Lay out your website for others to see it as a whole. If you aren't designing this on screen, then lay out your pages in the order of the buttons, with the home page first.

Development as a group

Your teacher will give each group an evaluation form so that you can evaluate another group's website (**Worksheet 49**). It is important to be fair.

Feed back to the class your comments on the website you have evaluated. The website with the highest score is the winner.

Plenary

Write on your whiteboards three key elements that made the winning website so successful. See if there is agreement on deciding what these elements are.

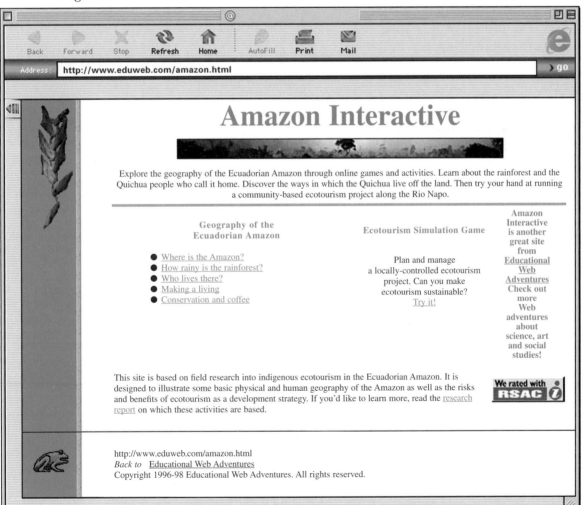

Address: http://www.eduweb.com/amazon.html

Amazon Interactive

Explore the geography of the Ecuadorian Amazon through online games and activities. Learn about the rainforest and the Quichua people who call it home. Discover the ways in which the Quichua live off the land. Then try your hand at running a community-based ecotourism project along the Rio Napo.

Geography of the Ecuadorian Amazon

- Where is the Amazon?
- How rainy is the rainforest?
- Who lives there?
- Making a living
- Conservation and coffee

Ecotourism Simulation Game

Plan and manage a locally-controlled ecotourism project. Can you make ecotourism sustainable?
Try it!

Amazon Interactive is another great site from Educational Web Adventures Check out more Web adventures about science, art and social studies!

This site is based on field research into indigenous ecotourism in the Ecuadorian Amazon. It is designed to illustrate some basic physical and human geography of the Amazon as well as the risks and benefits of ecotourism as a development strategy. If you'd like to learn more, read the research report on which these activities are based.

We rated with
RSAC *i*

http://www.eduweb.com/amazon.html
Back to Educational Web Adventures
Copyright 1996-98 Educational Web Adventures. All rights reserved.

Reviewing what's been learnt

By completing the work in this section you have explored and developed a range of important skills.

These include:

- Appreciating how, 400 years ago, Shakespeare created a drama that has the power to captivate a modern audience.

- Understanding the intensity of Shakespeare's language and imagery.

- Gaining an insight into the way in which a playwright's skill can allow different interpretations of the characters' motives.

- Considering the elements which help to make a drama successful and enduring.

Through your participation in the Website Challenge you have learnt how to:

- Find and select information from a range of sources.

- Navigate your way through the Internet successfully.

- Present information in a way that is accurate and appropriate, suiting your reader and purpose.

- Create a website that is appealing and accessible.

- Use presentational devices to good effect.

Developing these skills will be invaluable to you, whatever subjects you study and whatever career you pursue in the future.

Now it's time to think about what things you have learnt from this section and list the key points in your book, using the following sentence starters to help you:

- The things I found most interesting were ...

- The things I found most difficult were ...

- The things I think I did best were ...

- I now feel more confident about ...

- My targets to improve my work are: (include reading, writing, spelling, speaking and listening)
  -
  -
  -
  -
  -
  -

Persuade, argue, advise

Introduction

The structure and style that we write in today has been greatly influenced by how writing styles have developed over the centuries. Great writers, whose influence has lasted well beyond their times, exist in all cultures with a written heritage. In the United Kingdom we may count as part of the English literary heritage writers like William Shakespeare, John Donne, Jane Austen, Charles Dickens, Samuel Taylor Coleridge and Charlotte Brontë whose powers of expression and insights into the nature of humanity make their writing transcend time and culture and communicate to people world-wide.

In this section you will be looking at what such writers had to say, how it was linked to their immediate historical context, and how they said it in such a powerful and persuasive way as to communicate across the centuries. Using the appropriate terminology, you will be discussing their ideas and how they expressed them. You will also be thinking about the difficulties of conveying some of these great stories in film form instead of print, and writing advice for film producers.

Then you will consider how changes in the media are altering the way in which politicians try to persuade the public to support them, by examining how they use the techniques of advertising. In particular, you will be looking at the rhetorical devices used by contemporary political parties. You will focus on what the three main political parties have to say about crime and, using facts and figures gathered from an election briefing, write your own letter on this subject to a newspaper in the appropriate well-argued, persuasive style. Then you will learn a little about interview technique and, finally, have a go at doing your own spoof political propaganda for a youth party.

Key aims

In this section you will:

- Understand more about some of the great writers in English and why their work has maintained its appeal over the centuries.
- Look at how politicians and others use rhetorical devices for persuasion and how you can join your ideas together effectively when presenting an argument.

John Donne, poet and preacher

Aims

On these two pages you will:

- Think about why John Donne is part of our literary heritage and what we can learn about ideas which were current at the time he wrote 'The Sunne Rising'.
- Discuss, using the appropriate terminology, the ingredients which make 'The Sunne Rising' so effective.
- Analyse the use Donne makes of rhetorical devices.
- See how many great writers of English you recognize.

Starter *as a group*

You will have heard of a lot of famous writers and their writings (sometimes referred to as our 'literary heritage'). Some of them you will know through films, or you may have read extracts from their writing or seen references to them. Your teacher will give you the names of 12 writers who are considered to be part of the English literary heritage and the title of 12 famous works of theirs **(Worksheet 50)**. First, put to one side all the names that you have not heard of. Then see whether you can put the remaining names into chronological order. How many of the writers can you match with their work?

Introduction *as a class*

The poet and preacher John Donne (1572–1631) is a perfect writer to begin with when thinking about how great writers relate to their historical context. John Donne, a contemporary of Shakespeare, wrote 'The Sunne Rising' in 1603. He was also a contemporary of Galileo and many other great thinkers who have become known as part of the Renaissance, the rebirth of thinking following the restrictions on thought of medieval times. His poetry is alive with the philosophical and intellectual inquiry that dominated this age. Donne, and other poets of his time, loved to express ideas through **conceits** and **rhetorical devices** which won them the name of the **Metaphysical poets**.

Donne is famous both for his love poems and his religious poems. Today you're going to see how much you can understand, unaided, about one of his most famous love poems. Your teacher will read you the whole poem and then allocate different verses to different groups to work on. Listen carefully to how the poem is read, as this will provide many clues. While you listen you can work out the following:

- Who is speaking in the poem?
- Who is the speaker talking to?
- Who is the speaker with?

Discuss these as a class before working in groups.

---

conceit an elaborate image or startling comparison

Metaphysical poets a group of 17th-century poets whose poems tended to be in the form of a dramatic argument, often using outrageous logic

rhetorical devices techniques used to persuade an audience or reader

as a group

Each group should be prepared to give feedback about their verse on the following points:

1 Explain in your own words what you think Donne is saying in this verse.

2 Are there any words you can't understand?

3 Which lines do you think are the most effective – why?

THE SUNNE RISING

Busie old foole, unruly Sunne,
Why dost thou thus,
Through windowes, and through curtaines call on us?
Must to thy motions lovers seasons run?
Sawcy <u>pedantique</u>[1] wretch, goe chide
Late schoole boyes, and sowre <u>prentices</u>[2]
Goe tell Court-huntsmen that <u>the King will ride</u>,[3]
Call countrey ants to harvest offices;
Love, all alike, no season knowes, nor <u>clyme</u>,[4]
Nor houres, dayes, months, which are the rags of time.

Thy beames, so reverend, and strong
Why shouldst thou thinke?
I could eclipse and cloud them with a winke,
But that I would not lose her sight so long:
If her eyes have not blinded thine,
Looke, and to morrow late, tell mee,
Whether both <u>the'India's of spice</u>[5] and Myne
Be where thou leftst them, or lie here with mee.
Aske for those Kings whom thou saw'st yesterday,
And thou shalt heare, All here in one bed lay.

She'is all States, and all Princes, I.
Nothing else is.
Princes doe but play us; compar'd to this,
All honor's mimique; All wealth <u>alchimie</u>.[6]
Thou sunne art halfe as happy'as wee,
In that the world's contracted thus;
Thine age asks ease, and since thy duties bee
To warme the world, that's done in warming us.
Shine here to us, and thou art every where;
This bed thy center is, these walls thy <u>spheare</u>.[7]

Development
as a class

Discuss the following questions:

1 How has Donne linked his ideas throughout the poem?

2 Which of the following poetic techniques has he used significantly:

- Simile
- Metaphor
- Personification
- Conceit
- Alliteration
- Rhyme
- Rhythm
- Onomatopoeia?

3 What features make the poem persuasive? Consider the use of questions, the quality of the argument and the strength of feeling expressed.

Plenary

What aspects of this poem may have contributed to Donne's reputation as a world-class poet who is part of the English literary heritage?

[1] *pedantic, relying too much on academic learning*
[2] *apprentices*
[3] *James 1, who was King in 1603, loved hunting*
[4] *climate*
[5] *trade was increasing as more and more of the world was being discovered*
[6] *a scientific search to see whether cheap metals could be transformed into gold*
[7] *there was much intellectual debate about the movement of the planets (often referred to as spheres) and the relationship between the Earth and the Sun*

Aims

On these two pages you will:

- Use your skills in analysing text to decide why the opening of *Pride and Prejudice* is one of the best-known openings to a novel.
- Think about why Jane Austen is part of our literary heritage and discuss how her work relates to its historical context.

Starter *as a class*

Historians value the work of John Donne because his poetry gives insights into thought in his time. Jane Austen is also greatly valued by historians because her novels provide a detailed insight into a certain lifestyle. She was not trying to write about the great thoughts or events of her day but referred to the focus of her writing as 'the little bit of ivory on which I work with so fine a brush'. The area on which she focused so carefully was what life was like for the lower landed gentry – that is, those whose country estates were just about large enough to allow them to live in the style of the country gentleman.

If you were the eldest son in such a world, you would inherit the family estate and could contemplate a life of hunting, shooting and fishing, and going to a neighbouring spa or big city for 'the season' when balls were held to enable the right class of people to meet each other. As long as you managed to marry a woman with money, you would be able to continue to live in style. If you were a younger son, your horizons were limited to a

respectable profession which, for the gentry, meant you could either be a vicar or an officer in the army. If you were the eldest daughter, you could rely on a decent dowry (the property a woman brings to her husband on her marriage) and thus your marriage chances were good. You would have had the title 'Miss' to let prospective husbands know that you were the daughter with the money. If you were a younger daughter, you just had to hope that your beauty was sufficient to attract a man of wealth who was willing to make an 'imprudent' marriage. There was no concept of a career for women. A woman's future was to be a wife – not marrying was to be feared. You would have spent your time playing the piano, singing, doing needlework and keeping out of the sun (very pale skin was a sign of being genteel).

as a group

In your groups discuss:

1. What the difficulties facing a young man growing up in such a world would be.
2. What the difficulties facing a young woman growing up in such a world would be.
3. The meanings of 'imprudent' and 'prospective' in the context of the passage. Can you think of any other words that include the roots 'prudent' or 'spect'?

Be prepared to discuss your conclusions.

> Jane Austen (1775–1817) is one of Britain's most respected novelists. She wrote *Pride and Prejudice, Mansfield Park, Emma, Northanger Abbey, Persuasion* and *Sense and Sensibility*.

Introduction *as a group*

Flex your PECs (see page 34). As you know, literary analysis is all about being able to make a point, having the evidence to back it up, and the confidence to comment on its significance. So let's get in training by analysing Jane Austen's writing style. Listen carefully to the opening of her novel *Pride and Prejudice* (**Worksheets 51a–b**).

Discuss the following questions. Use **Worksheet 52** to help you jot down your ideas.

1   What is the tone of the first two paragraphs? Is the author being serious or wanting to entertain her readers?

2   How can you tell that this is not a genteel, 21st-century couple speaking?

3   What do you learn about Mrs Bennet's character from this chapter?

4   What do you learn about Mr Bennet's character from this chapter?

5   What clues are there for how the plot will develop?

Be prepared to discuss your ideas with the class.

It is a truth universally acknowledged, that a single man in possession of a good fortune, must be in want of a wife.

However little known the feelings or views of such a man may be on his first entering the neighbourhood, this truth is so well fixed in the minds of the surrounding families, that he is considered as the rightful property of some one or other of their daughters.

Development *as a class*

1   Are Mr and Mrs Bennet a happily married couple? What evidence do you have to support your answer?

2   Is Jane Austen at ease with the values of this world or is she challenging them? What evidence do you have to support your answer?

3   What makes Austen's characterization so effective?

4   Why do you think this passage has become one of the most famous openings to a novel ever written in any language?

Plenary

What features of the opening of this novel might persuade a reader to want to carry on reading?

Charles Dickens, novelist

Aims

On these two pages you will:

- Use your skills in text analysis to explain why the opening of *Great Expectations* is effective.
- Think about why Charles Dickens is part of our literary heritage and discuss how his work relates to its historical context.

Starter  on your own

Charles Dickens is one of the world's most famous novelists. Fill in the first column of the **KWL grid** on **Worksheet 53** to establish what, if anything, you already know about Charles Dickens.

> **KWL grid** a grid to help structure your thinking for a research project, which asks you what you already **K**now, what you **W**ant to know, and what you have **L**earnt at the end of the project

Introduction as a class

By the time Jane Austen died in 1817, the industrial revolution was in full swing, society was undergoing many changes and the pursuit of wealth had become a national obsession. Perhaps this, and the fact that Dickens' father had spent time in the debtors' prison, influenced Charles Dickens to seek a wider perspective than that selected by Jane Austen. He chose as his canvas the whole of society.

Hollywood and BBC Christmas productions of Dickens' novels have made us associate Dickens with cheery festive scenes in Victorian dress where the bad get their deserts and the good get their reward. Many of Dickens' early novels, like *Oliver Twist*, did have this simple moral message but his later novels increasingly reflect how haunted he was by a sense that the Victorian world, with its obsession about money, was developing in a way which was corrupting everyone. He was also haunted by the shame that he felt about his father. Moreover, Dickens' experiences of love made him all too aware that human emotions were not the simple 'and they lived happily ever after' affairs beloved of novelists.

Such guilt and sense of ill ease reoccurs throughout a whole range of characters in his novels but in none more effectively than *Great Expectations*, the ultimate story about the corrupting power of money. The orphan, Pip, is brought up by his mean, unloving sister, the wife of the blacksmith, Joe Gargery. In this novel the poor are no longer automatically good. Dickens' novels teem with characters and coincidences all serving, by parallel and contrast, to get his message across.

Great Expectations is written in an autobiographical style with the adult Pip relating his story. It begins with Pip's earliest memory of an event which was to change the course of his life. Listen carefully while your teacher reads you the opening chapter of *Great Expectations*. The extract begins on page 69 and continues on **Worksheets 54a–c**.

My father's family name being Pirrip, and my christian name Philip, my infant tongue could make of both names nothing longer or more explicit than Pip. So I called myself Pip, and came to be called Pip.

I give Pirrip as my father's family name, on the authority of his tombstone and my sister – Mrs. Joe Gargery, who married the blacksmith. As I never saw my father or my mother, and never saw any likeness either of them (for their days were long before the days of photographs) my first fancies of what they were like, were unreasonably derived from their tombstones. The shape of the letters on my father's, gave me an odd idea that he was a square, stout, dark man, with curly black hair. From the character and turn of the inscription, '*Also Georgina Wife of the Above*,' I drew a childish conclusion that my mother was freckled and sickly. To five little stone lozenges, each about a foot and a half long, which were arranged in a neat row beside their grave, and were sacred to the memory of five little brothers of mine – who gave up trying to get a living, exceedingly early in that universal struggle – I am indebted for a belief I religiously entertained that they had all been born on their backs with their hands in their trouserspockets, and had never taken them out in this state of existence.

as a group

Your teacher will give you some cards (**Worksheet 55**) which outline the structure of the opening chapter. Your task is to:

- Sequence the cards into the order Dickens chose to open his novel
- Decide what atmosphere Dickens was trying to create
- Decide what ingredients Dickens chose to include.

Charles Dickens (1812–1870) was a popular and prolific novelist. Many of his novels, including *Pickwick Papers*, *Oliver Twist*, *Nicholas Nickleby* and *David Copperfield*, were published in monthly instalments.

Development **as a class**

The story is being narrated by the adult Pip looking back on his life.

1 What do you learn about the personality of the adult Pip from the opening two paragraphs of the novel?

2 Just looking at these two paragraphs, what do you notice about how Dickens constructs his sentences?

Dickens builds up meaning and significance in his novels by relating his characters to the physical environment that surrounds them. In the extract on **Worksheets 54a–c** Pip is being physically attacked by the convict but the convict is also being attacked. Look at the fourth paragraph.

3 What is attacking the convict?

4 What effect does this have on our attitude toward the convict?

5 What evidence is there in this extract that the convict is scared?

Think about the last two paragraphs.

6 What image do you have of the convict from these paragraphs?

7 Why do you think Dickens has created this image of the convict?

Fill in the last column of your KWL grid and be prepared to present your points to the class.

Plenary

Sum up the qualities that make Dickens' writing so effective.

Advising film-makers

Aims

On these two pages you will:

- Comment on the ability of a film version of *Great Expectations* to recreate the atmosphere of the novel's opening scene, using the appropriate technical vocabulary.
- Write formal guidelines, advising film producers on how to adapt novels into film.

Starter

If you have ever read a story and loved it and then seen it as a film, you will be aware of how let down you can feel if the film version doesn't live up to the images in your own head. Discuss what problems face any film producer who wants to turn a well-loved novel into a film and what the possible advantages of film could be over a novel. Consider also the particular problems which would face any film-maker recreating the opening scene of *Great Expectations*. Use **Worksheet 56** to record the key points from your discussions. Be prepared to present your ideas to the class.

Introduction as a class

There have been three big-screen films made of Dickens' *Great Expectations* as well as many television productions. The most famous of the films, and many would argue the best, is the black and white version starring Alec Guinness. The most recent, starring Gwyneth Paltro and Robert De Niro, moves the action to modern times in America, changes Pip's name, the setting and the imagery that comes to symbolize the significance of events, and may make you wonder if you're watching the right film. Your teacher will show you the opening of one of these film or television versions. Discuss the following questions using the appropriate language of **critical analysis**. Note down the key points you wish to make for each question.

1 Has the film created a sense of a narrator looking back on his early childhood?

2 Has the film helped the viewer to see the world through the eyes of the young Pip?

3 Was the arrival of the convict scary? If so, what elements helped create this?

4 Does the film make you feel in any way sorry for the convict?

5 Is the way the convict introduces the 'young man' scary? If so, what elements helped create this?

6 What image of the convict are you left with by the end of the scene?

7 What are the key differences between Dickens' opening to *Great Expectations* and the film version?

8 What aspects make the film version effective or not?

9 Has the film-maker done a good job of recreating the essence of the opening scene?

critical analysis a way of analysing literature and commenting on it using technical terms

Development (on your own)

Your task now is to write some formal, impersonal advice to any film-maker who is contemplating creating a film version of a novel you have read and like. Use the following suggestions to help you structure your advice:

- Brainstorm all the points you want to make and jot them down
- Decide what would be the best order for these points
- Decide how you are going to introduce your bullet points.

Remember that bullet points should all follow on grammatically from the phrase that introduces them – in the list above, they all begin with a verb in the **imperative**.

> **imperative** the form of a verb used to give a command

Plenary

Discuss your two or three key pieces of advice to someone making a film version of a novel. See if the class can agree on the key points of advice. Note down any additional points that you may want to add to your draft.

homework

Compose the final draft of your advice to film-makers.

> **!** **Remember** to read through your draft and make any alterations to the structure, content, grammar or spelling which may be necessary to help your communication be more effective. Ensure that your advice is structured logically and flows coherently. When you have proofread your work, write a brief comment on how well you think you have completed the task.

Coleridge, poet and essayist

Aims

On these two pages you will:

- Use your skills in analysing text to explain why 'The Rime of the Ancient Mariner' is so powerful and why it has become part of our literary heritage.
- Consider why Coleridge is known as a Romantic poet.
- Use the appropriate technical terms to analyse the language of poetry.

Starter   *in pairs*

Writers rely on a range of devices to make their writing come alive. Poets are often most concerned to bring out images and sounds. Your teacher will give you a range of poetic terms (**Worksheet 57**) plus three headings. Your task is to group the terms under the following headings:

- Imagery
- Sound effects
- Structure of poem.

Once you have done this, see if you can explain how you have categorized the terms and define clearly what each term means. If possible, provide an example to help a listener understand. Be prepared to present your ideas to the class.

Introduction   *as a class*

It is the ability of a great artist to sum up the human condition that makes their work valued across the ages. Aspects of Dickens' life haunted him and helped feed his imagination which, in turn, fed the quality of his writing. Many of the best writers and artists have shared this sense of being haunted in some way. The last of the writers you are going to look at in this section is the poet Samuel Taylor Coleridge, who was born three years before Jane Austen. He summed up the nature of his life by writing his own disturbing epitaph.

Lift one thought in prayer for STC
That he, who many a year with toilsome breath,
Found Death in Life, may here find Life in Death.

Coleridge is classified as one of the **Romantic poets**, poets who, in the second half of the 18th century, focused on passion, mystery, imagination and creativity. However, like all great writers, Coleridge had his own unique way of expressing his ideas. One of his most famous poems is 'The Rime of the Ancient Mariner', which he wrote in an imaginary old English to create the atmosphere he wanted. It is a long ballad that tells the story of a sailor who is cursed by his evil action of shooting an albatross. His action brought ill luck and resulted in a long and painful death to all his colleagues, but the ancient mariner himself is condemned to a form of living death.

Romantic poets poets writing in the period from about 1789 to 1832, such as Coleridge and Wordsworth, who brought a new level of emotional intensity and imagination to their work

Once a year the mariner has to find a stranger and tell them his story – in this instance he selects a wedding guest.

On the surface, the poem appears to be the mysterious story of a sea voyage affected by supernatural powers, but it could also be a metaphor or symbol of mental breakdown, of a mind that races manically along and then suddenly despairs and cannot stir itself to any action. As Coleridge expresses it in one of the last verses in the poem:

O Wedding-Guest! this soul hath been
Alone on a wide wide sea:
So lonely 'twas, that God himself
Scarce seemed there to be.

Listen to the sound and power of the poem as your teacher reads you a passage from one of the greatest stories ever told, 'The Rime of the Ancient Mariner' (**Worksheet 58**).

as a group

Your task is to decide what ingredients make the poem powerful. Be prepared to present your ideas to the class.

1 Select the ingredients from those you have sorted in the starter activity.

2 Add any additional ingredients you think are needed – use the blank cards from the starter.

3 Annotate one copy of the text so that you have the evidence to back up your points.

4 Decide which verse you think is the most effective.

Development **as a class**

1 Listen carefully as each group presents their 'ingredients'. Join in the discussion so that, as a class, you can build up a list and note the evidence for what makes this passage so powerful.

2 Look back at the qualities of the Romantic poets given in the introduction. Does this poem fit those categories?

Plenary

Why do you think several famous artists have chosen to illustrate this poem?

Why do you think Samuel Taylor Coleridge is considered part of the English literary heritage?

homework

In this section you have looked at extracts from the work of four great writers. Add them to your reading record and decide whether you want to try to read more by any of these writers. Look back at the reading targets you set yourself at the beginning of the year (see page 16) and any more recent reading targets you have set. Decide whether you have achieved your targets and what your targets now need to be.

Politics as advertising

Aims

On these two pages you will:

- Analyse and discuss the use made of rhetorical devices in political propaganda.
- Compare the presentation of ideas and values.
- Listen to conflicting points of view, identifying similarities and differences, and weigh up the evidence to reach a conclusion.
- Analyse the way a writer opens, develops and completes his paragraphs in a passage of polemic.

Starter *as a class*

In 1985 Neil Postman, an American professor of communications, wrote his **polemic** *Amusing Ourselves to Death*, in which he argued that television is transforming our culture into one vast arena for show business in which all public affairs (including politics, religion, news, education, journalism and commerce) have been turned into a form of entertainment. It is an urgent plea for us to question what is happening before it is too late. Your teacher will give you the opening paragraphs to the chapter on politics entitled 'Reach Out and Elect Someone' (**Worksheet 59**). Listen carefully while your teacher reads you the extract and analyses the structure of the first paragraph for you.

> Rhetorical device of using the opening paragraph as a hook to get reader interested in the topic under discussion. Begins with easily understandable and interesting ideas to try to involve reader.

In *The Last Hurrah*, Edwin O'Connor's fine novel about lusty party politics in Boston, Mayor Frank Skeffington tries to instruct his young nephew in the realities of political machinery. Politics, he tells him, is the greatest spectator sport in America. In 1996, Ronald Reagan used a different metaphor. "Politics," he said, "is just like show business."

> Brief quotation to help make his point come alive.

> Gets reader thinking about images that politics has been compared to in preparation for what he is to say in this chapter. Paragraph links the O'Connor sport comparison to Reagan's show business comparison through the connecting phrase 'used a different metaphor'.

 in pairs

Your teacher will give you one paragraph to focus on but, to understand and analyse your paragraph, you need to consider it within the context of the whole passage. Remember to refer to the context and **morphology** to work out the meaning of any unfamiliar words.

Discuss the following points and be prepared to present your ideas to the class.

1 In the paragraph you are focusing on, analyse how Postman has linked his ideas and list any rhetorical devices used. Annotate your paragraph so that you can present it to the class.

2 Think about how Postman has used connectives to link the paragraph you are focusing on to the previous one.

3 Consider how he has introduced, developed and concluded his ideas in this paragraph.

4 See how he is preparing the ground for the next paragraph.

as a class

Listen to and discuss the ideas that each group feeds back and then decide what Postman is saying about politics.

> **morphology** the consistent patterns of letters that make up words
> **polemic** a controversial discussion

Introduction

In the run-up to the June 2001 general election, the Conservative Party leader was endlessly accusing the Labour Party leader of empty spin (fine-sounding, meaningless nothings). Do all of the main political parties in Britain use the same rhetorical and stylistic devices or are there stylistic differences between them?

as a group

Working in groups of six, you will be given the text from the opening page of the web entry for each of the three main political party election manifestos (**Worksheets 60a–b**), plus three copies of the analysis grid (**Worksheet 61**), which lists a range of rhetorical and stylistic devices. Divide into three pairs. Each pair should focus on a different political party and use the analysis grid to see whether they can find evidence in the manifesto they are focusing on for each of the rhetorical and stylistic devices listed on the grid. Read your text out loud to each other before filling in the grid.

Development as a group

Once each pair has completed their analysis, come together as a group and decide if all the parties were using the same devices. Discuss how effective the rhetorical devices are. Be prepared to present your findings to the rest of the class. Ensure that you have evidence to back up your points.

as a class

Each group should sum up its key findings and be ready to support its conclusions with evidence. Can the class agree on its analysis or are there differing interpretations?

Plenary

What evidence have you established to support or disprove Neil Postman's argument that politics today is like advertising?

Your family – the family manifesto

A Real Chance for Real Change

It's time for **common sense**

The politics of crime

Aims

On these two pages you will:

- Compare points of view.
- See if you can analyse bias when listening to a text.
- Recognize underlying themes and issues and weigh up the evidence to reach a conclusion.
- Analyse how paragraphs in the election briefing have been introduced, developed, linked and concluded.

Starter as a class

Follow carefully while your teacher reads you the **election briefing** 'How the parties differ over … crime' from the magazine *The Week* published on 2 June 2001 (**Worksheet 62**). Try to analyse how the political parties differ over crime. Next lesson, you will be doing your own writing on this topic. The more you listen today, the easier the writing task will be.

Be prepared to discuss the following questions:

1 What technique has the writer used to introduce each paragraph?

2 Does this technique help link the paragraphs effectively?

3 Re-read the third paragraph carefully. Consider how the writer has developed and concluded the argument and how evidence has been used to support the points made.

4 Is this paragraph well constructed? be prepared to provide evidence for your answer.

5 Do you think the article is **biased** towards any of the political parties?

> **biased** unfairly favouring one viewpoint over another
> **election briefing** a weighing up of the political parties' policies prior to an election

Introduction as a group

Your teacher will divide the class up into three groups. Group 1 will analyse the Conservative Party's approach to crime, Group 2 will analyse the Labour Party's approach and the last group will look at the approach taken by the Liberal Democrats. Everyone in each group will have the first 200 or so words of their party's approach to crime (**Worksheets 63a–c**), taken from the party websites, plus copies of the analysis grid (**Worksheet 64**) to sum up how each party chose to present its policy on crime. Working in pairs within your group, read your allocated party's statement on crime and fill in the first section of the analysis grid which focuses on bias. Now confer with the rest of your group and come to a consensus.

Your next task is to select a representative from your group who will read your extract to the rest of the class. As the class listen (they will not have a copy of the text), your group representative should ask them to try to spot any examples of bias. See if they draw the same conclusions as your group. Excerpts may need to be re-read to them and the class should be encouraged to give their views.

Conservatives.com

Register Keep Up to Date Feedback Donate Volunteer Join Party Send to a Friend

■ Home
■ News
■ Campaigns
■ Speeches
■ People
■ The Party
■ Members
■ Conference
■ PDA / WAP

Log In
Email or ID:

Password: go

Search Keyword
                             go

time for **common sense**
the Conservative manifesto

through **our lives**
▶*raising* **a family**
▶*living* **safely**
▶*earning* **a living**
▶*staying* **healthy**
▶*growing* **older**

knowing **who we are**
▶*a* **world leader**
▶*a* **stronger society**
▶*town and* **country**
▶*a* **civilised country**
▶*a proud* **democracy**

through **our lives**
living **safely**

Common sense means having enough police to keep our streets safe and a criminal justice system that reflects our values rather than undermines them

- Increase police numbers
- Free police from bureaucracy so that they can get on with policing
- Take persistent young offenders off our streets
- Criminals to serve the sentence given by the court
- More rights for victims

Internet zone

Development *as a class*

1 Listen carefully while a representative from each group presents their text to the class. Listen for:
   - Examples of bias
   - Key arguments
   - Key points of policy.

Fill in the final two sections of the analysis grid.

2 Each group helps lead the discussion on their text. See whether the whole class can agree on:
   - The level of bias in each case
   - Key arguments in each case
   - Key points of policy in each case.

3 Once you have heard all three party approaches, consider the following overall implications:
   - The key areas of difference between the parties' policies on crime
   - Whether the parties agree on any aspect of how to deal with crime.

Plenary

Was *The Week* accurate in the way it summed up the party positions? Give reasons to support your choice.

Letter to the editor

Aims

On these two pages you will:

- Analyse the use made of rhetorical devices in a letter to the editor.
- Write a persuasive letter about a controversial issue, countering arguments and offering alternatives.
- Shape your ideas rapidly into cohesive paragraphs and evaluate your ability to do this.

Starter  in pairs

This is today's key task:

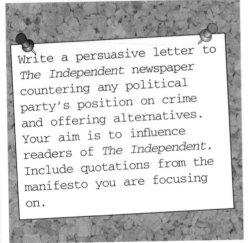

Write a persuasive letter to *The Independent* newspaper countering any political party's position on crime and offering alternatives. Your aim is to influence readers of *The Independent*. Include quotations from the manifesto you are focusing on.

First, look at what a letter to the editor of *The Independent* is like. Listen carefully while your teacher reads you the letter on **Worksheet 65** and be prepared to answer the following questions:

1. What rhetorical devices has the writer used to try to influence the audience?
2. Is the writer concerned about being biased?
3. What emotive language is used?
4. Are some words used ironically?

Introduction on your own

As you have noticed, the writer of the letter was sufficiently annoyed by what they had read in *The Independent* about public apathy to be motivated to write to the paper and put a different perspective as persuasively as possible.

Now it's your turn. Select whichever of the political parties' manifestos on crime most irritated you (**Worksheets 63a–c**) and write a letter to *The Independent* explaining just how inadequate that party's policy on crime is. Refer also to the article from *The Week* (**Worksheet 62**) to provide you with ammunition for your arguments. If you don't feel irritated by any of the party's perspectives on crime, then write your letter in the persona of someone who does.

Consider each of these points before you draft your letter:

1. You know what your *purpose* is – to ridicule one party's approach to tackling crime.

2. You know who the *audience* is – readers of *The Independent*.

3. So now you need to consider *content*. Decide exactly what you want to say. Highlight the points from the crime manifesto that you want to attack and decide which extracts you are going to quote. Organize the evidence to back up your points. Remember that you have to counter the arguments that have been expressed, address the weaknesses and offer alternatives.

4. Now think about *structure*. How will you order your points? Write the heading for each point on a small piece of paper or a post-it note and move them around until the order seems right.

5 And, finally, consider *style*. Think about the way you are going to make your points. Remember to use rhetorical devices like:

- Rhetorical questions
- Indignant tone
- Emotive language that mocks your opponent
- Irony
- Direct appeals to readers to support your views
- Use of 'we' to suggest the masses are with you
- Exaggeration.

6 You may want to use some of the following openers to set the right tone for your indignation:

This is just the sort of …

It's about time …

Are they seriously arguing that …

Any sensible person would …

A child could recognize that …

If you think…

Do we really have to…

Development *on your own*

Now it's time to begin. If you are role-playing your indignation then get in role. If you are genuinely indignant, be indignant. As you start to write, imagine this indignant person spitting out their points and chuckling as they amass evidence that will destroy their opponents' arguments. If you have prepared well, your letter should now flow and you should be able to shape your ideas rapidly into **cohesive** paragraphs.

When you have finished the first draft, read it through and rework those sentences to maximize their effectiveness. Once you are pleased with your draft, swap with a partner and help each other to firm up your arguments.

> **cohesive** a cohesive text is one whose parts fit well together. This is often signposted by grammatical features such as connectives.

Plenary

Listen while a few class members read out the opening of their letters. Discuss which rhetorical devices seem to have worked best so far.

homework

Read your draft out loud and see if the sentences flow effectively. Check that you have used evidence to back up your perspective. Write a final draft.

> **!** **Remember** to give your letter a quick read through out loud to check that it works and then make any final adjustments. Proofread it carefully and write a brief comment saying how well you think you have completed the task. Focus particularly on whether you think you managed to shape your ideas rapidly into cohesive paragraphs. Set a target for yourself to improve this aspect of your work.

Interviewing techniques

Aims

On these two pages you will:
- Develop interview techniques which will help an interviewee to express themselves.
- Offer advice to an interviewer.

Starter  in pairs

Today you are going to interview your partner and try to help them express clearly and **coherently** their views on crime. Many of the interviews that you see on television, especially those with professional politicians, are very cut-throat; the interviewer's aim is to bring out the inadequacies of their guest's arguments. The most aggressive of the television interviewers is probably Jeremy Paxman who will say things to his victims like:

A very different, much more positive, interviewing style is where the interviewer encourages the interviewee to express themselves coherently. Listen carefully while your teacher and a member of the class present the extract (right) from the opening of an interview with television celebrity and actress Oprah Winfrey.

This was televised in 1998 when she was interviewed about *Beloved*, a film she had just starred in based on a book of the same name by Toni Morrison. Pay particular attention to how the interviewer has framed the questions.

> **coherent** text is coherent if the ideas expressed are relevant to each other and are presented in a logical way so that the reader can follow the meaning

Interview with Oprah

INTERVIEWER: You obviously believe in the power of the image. How do you think a film version of *Beloved* will affect people in a way that the book didn't?

OPRAH WINFREY: Oh, good question. When I finished the book, because I am a thoroughbred reader – I call myself a thoroughbred reader – I felt that this was an occasion where the book did more than most books do. Most books tell you a story and let you see what a person's life is like. What *Beloved* did was let you feel what a person's life was like. And feel the exhaustion and devastation of slavery and its impact on one person's life. And the lives of the people who surrounded her. That's what *Beloved* did ... you felt it. That's why I wanted to do the movie. Because I wanted people to feel that. If I had a book club, I probably wouldn't have done the movie ...

1 Decide what techniques the interviewer has used to help the speaker present themselves favourably.

2 Can you think of any other techniques or phrases that they could have used to help the speaker?

3 Draw up a bullet point list of advice for would-be interviewers to help them interview sympathetically. You might want to include a list of don'ts as well as dos.

INTERVIEWER: Did you attempt to alter anything or bring anything additional or different to the audience?

OPRAH WINFREY: We're pretty faithful to that book. We just wanted to tell the story and to be as faithful as possible. I'm a reader and I don't go to a lot of movies, but I mostly love movies that are turned from books, 'cause that's what I do. And I just felt like nobody in the world's been more faithful to a book than we have …

INTERVIEWER: So, when was the last time you read it [Beloved]?

OPRAH WINFREY: I haven't read it since the movie. I read it almost every day during the movie. It was our *Bible* during the movie, we carried it around every day. I read it before I started doing the movie. I read it again and literally pulled out every scene <u>Sethe</u>[1] had. Anything. [I] went through the book, line by line, and any scene or thought that could contribute to how Sethe would feel about herself, or how she would react, I would pull all of that out.

Introduction *in pairs*

A documentary about crime is being prepared for television and your partner, because of their letter published in *The Independent*, has been chosen to present their views on the programme. You are the interviewer. Your brief is to interview your partner as sympathetically as possible to help draw out their views.

- What have you just learnt about what techniques to use?
- If you receive a one-word or very short reply, what should you do?

Read your partner's letter carefully and work out what the main issues are. Then decide which points you will attempt to draw out. Jot down your points and make sure that they are in a logical order. Take it in turns to have a trial run at attempting to put your interview strategy into practice. Help each other to be better interviewers and interviewees.

Development *as a group*

Join with another pair and take it in turns to be the interviewer, the interviewee or the audience. After each interview, the audience can offer up to two pieces of advice to the interviewer and the interviewee. When all four interviews have taken place, see whether you can agree on which was the most effective and why. Your teacher will be coming round to see which interviews are working well.

Plenary

What elements made the successful interviews successful?

[1] the character Oprah Winfrey played in the film

Vote for me

Aims

On these two pages you will:

- Discuss how bullet points should be used effectively as a presentational device and write advice in bullet point format.
- Exploit the stylistic conventions of a persuasive campaign leaflet and write a parody of one.

Starter  in pairs

Residents in Brixton, south London, like most areas of the country, received a wide range of political leaflets during the campaign leading up to the June 2001 general election, including a leaflet from the Socialist Alliance. The extract on the right is taken from that leaflet. Read the list of bullet points and discuss the following three questions:

1. How many of the bullet points actually follow on grammatically from the opening statement, 'We stand for'? What difference does this make?

2. What is the logic of the order in which the points have been put and presented in bold? Does this matter?

3. There are 15 bullet points in this list. Is that about the right number?

We stand for

- **Stop privatisation – renationalise the railways**
- Tax the rich and big business to rebuild the welfare state
- **For the right to work – 35 hour-week now**
- Defend asylum seekers
- **End discrimination. Oppose racism, sexism and homophobia**
- A fully-funded NHS. End privatisation and cuts
- **Raise pensions and restore the link with earnings**
- Stop the sell off of council houses. End homelessness.
- **Fully-funded comprehensive education. No selection**
- Strengthen trade union rights in the workplace
- **Raise the minimum wage to £7 per hour – the European union decency threshold**
- Save the planet – we want tough action on pollution and food safety
- **Scrap tuition fees – free high-quality education for all**
- Stop the onslaught on civil rights
- **Cancel third world debt**

What advice would you give to would-be users of bullet points? Express this advice formally in bullet points on your whiteboard or a piece of paper. Be prepared to present your advice to the class.

Introduction `in pairs`

Elections often encourage joke candidates to stand. The most famous recent example was the late Screaming Lord Sutch who represented the Monster Raving Loony Party.

Many young people think that politicians don't consider them because they don't have the vote. This is your chance to remedy this situation. In pairs, invent your own **spoof** young people's political party and write its campaign leaflet, parodying the style of contemporary political leaflets.

1. Consider the content of your leaflet. Think of all the things that young people would like – don't worry about realism, just go for it.

2. Consider the style of the language you will use. Remember the features you identified in the three main parties' political propaganda and write your manifesto exaggerating that same style:

   - **Sound bites** which could be from adverts
   - Repetition
   - Short simple sentences
   - Ideas linked by repetition not logic

sound bite information that is packaged in a few words so that it fits nicely into very short interviews

spoof a mildly satirical mockery or parody

- Meaningless, grand-sounding claims
- Use of a personal approach from the party leader
- Direct appeal to voters.

Remember to follow your own bullet point advice. Or, you could decide to copy the bullet point style of the starter activity to maximize the humour of your spoof leaflet. Use your whiteboard to draft a few ideas.

Development `in pairs`

Now draft your leaflet. Remember to keep text to a minimum. Sketch the design for your leaflet. What text will be in large type? What will be your leading sound bite? What images will accompany your leaflet? Don't worry if you can't draw. Just sketch in the ideas – it's the ideas that count, not the artistic ability.

Plenary

Your teacher will select a few students to present their draft leaflets to the class. What features have made them successful?

homework

Finalize your draft leaflet.

> **!** **Remember** to focus on the ideas and how to present them rather than on trying to produce an artistically excellent product. When you have finished, give your leaflet a final proof-read to check that it is an effective spoof of a political leaflet. Then write a comment on how well you think you have completed this task.

Reviewing what's been learnt

In this section you have focused on extracts from the work of some of the great writers who make up the English literary heritage. You have seen how their work relates to the age in which it was written and considered what it is about their work that has helped it maintain its appeal over the centuries. You have also written advice to film producers when they turn great novels into film.

Then you looked at the language of politics and how politicians and others use rhetorical devices to persuade. You compared the three main parties' approach to the issue of crime, and wrote your own letter to an editor on the issue in the appropriate persuasive style. You practised interviewing techniques where the questions are intended to help the speaker answer coherently and, finally, you wrote your own spoof party leaflet outlining your manifesto for youth.

Now it's time to think about what things you have learnt from this section and list the key points in your book, using the following sentence starters to help you:

- The things I found most interesting were ...
- The things I found most difficult were ...
- The things I think I did best were ...
- I now feel more confident about ...

My targets to improve my work are

Reading: This section required some sophisticated analysis of text including comparing ideas, analysing rhetorical devices and considering what are the ingredients of effective writing. Look back at your last reading target review (homework, page 73) and decide what your targets now need to be.
-
-

Writing: How well did you manage to argue a case persuasively or counter a view? Did you manage to shape ideas rapidly in cohesive paragraphs? Are you confident about expressing advice coherently? Decide what your targets now need to be.
-
-

Spelling: Which type of words are still causing you problems? Look at your spelling log and decide what your spelling targets need to be.
-
-

Speaking and listening: How well did you cope with being a supportive interviewer? When listening, could you compare and identify different points of view, and recognize underlying themes and implications? Could you analyse bias and discuss and evaluate different evidence? Decide what your speaking and listening targets now need to be.
-
-

Analyse, review, comment

Introduction

In the first half of this section you will be looking at extracts from three different playscripts. They are separated by over 200 years but all include as part of their purpose a strong element of social comment or satire. Two of them are also very funny. To begin with you will be analysing the language, structure and dramatic techniques of the scripts, and thinking about the craft of the playwrights and what skills the actors and directors need to bring to them. Then you will use these skills to improvise your own scene and develop this into a scripted scene which you will present.

Later in the section you will turn your attention to three different kinds of journalism: the theatre review, the celebrity interview and the 'analysis' article. You will be looking at what kind of writing is appropriate for each genre and attempting to write your own. You will be involved in activities throughout the section which explore different attitudes to language, both spoken and written. By the end of the section, when you write a newspaper article on slang, you will have a very good idea about the different levels of formality that exist in English and the appropriate uses of each type.

Key aims

In this section you will:

- Develop your skills in analysing, reviewing and commenting on drama, as well as working in a group to write, direct and perform a script.

- Examine different kinds of newspaper and magazine articles, thinking carefully about the formality of the language used, and write your own article.

CAPTAIN ABSOLUTE (*reads*) *As for the old weather-beaten she-dragon who guards you* – Who can he mean by that?

MRS MALAPROP Me, sir! – me! – he means me! – There – what do you think now? – but go on a little further.

CAPTAIN ABSOLUTE Impudent scoundrel! – (*reads*) *I will elude her vigilance, as I am told that the same ridiculous vanity, which makes her dress up her coarse features, and deck her dull chat with hard words which she don't understand* –

DIRECT FROM BROADWAY

PERFORMANCE

THE RIVALS
Salisbury Playhouse

Thursday September 6–Saturday 29 at 8pm

Sheridan's top quipping Restoration comedy – all mistaken identity and improbable outcomes from the scribbler of School for Scandal. Set in Georgian Bath and featuring the legendary word-mangler Mrs Malaprop.

PEGGY SUE GOT MARRIED

Attitudes to English in Pygmalion

Aims

On these two pages you will:

- Analyse the language, form and dramatic impact of two scenes from Shaw's *Pygmalion*.
- Explore different attitudes to the use of accent and dialect in English, in particular comparing regional dialects with Standard English.

Starter  as a class

George Bernard Shaw's play *Pygmalion*, as well as being very funny, is also a satire on our attitudes to language and class. Later this lesson you will be looking in more detail at one scene of the play. To begin with, read together a short extract from Act 1 (right), in which a group of people are sheltering from the rain in Covent Garden, London. Liza is a flower-seller; Freddy, a middle-class young man, has just collided with her; and the scene is watched by Henry Higgins, a linguist, who is making notes on everyone's accents.

George Bernard Shaw (1856–1950), Irish dramatist and critic, wrote several major satirical plays, including *Pygmalion* (1913) which was adapted as the musical play *My Fair Lady* in 1956. Shaw was also an active socialist and a passionate advocate of spelling reform.

LIZA   Nah then, Freddy: look wh' y' gowin, deah.

FREDDY   Sorry (*he rushes off*).

LIZA   (*picking up her scattered flowers and replacing them in the basket*) There's menners f' yer! Tə-oo[1] banches of voylets trod into the mad.

MRS EYNSFORD HILL   How do you know that my son's name is Freddy, pray?

LIZA   Ow, eez, yə-ooa san, is e? Wal, fewd dan y'dooty bawmz a mather should, eed now bettern to spawl a pore gel's flahrzn than ran away athaht pyin. Will ye-oo py me f'them? (*Here, with apologies, this desperate attempt to represent her dialect without a* <u>phonetic alphabet</u>[2] *must be abandoned as unintelligible outside London.*) …

HIGGINS   A woman who utters such depressing and disgusting sounds has no right to be anywhere – no right to live. Remember that you are a human being with a soul and the divine gift of <u>articulate</u>[3] speech: that your native language is the language of Shakespeare and Milton and The Bible; and don't sit there crooning like a bilious pigeon.

LIZA   (*quite overwhelmed, looking up at him in mingled wonder and* <u>deprecation</u>[4] *without daring to raise her head*) Ah-ah-ah-ow-ow-ow-oo!

HIGGINS   (*whipping out his book*) Heavens! what a sound! (*He writes; then holds out the book and reads, reproducing her vowels exactly*) Ah-ah-ah-ow-ow-ow-oo!

LIZA   (*tickled by the performance, and laughing in spite of herself*) Garn!

[1] *Shaw used an upside-down e to indicate the neutral vowel sound, as in the word 'the'*
[2] *an alphabet in which the letters match the pronunciation exactly*
[3] *fluent, well-constructed*
[4] *disapproval*

Discuss the following questions as a class:

1. What is Higgins's attitude to Liza's Cockney accent?

2. Name or describe two or three other regional accents and dialects. Do you think Higgins would have felt the same about them as he did about Cockney?

3 *Pygmalion* was written in 1913. What attitudes are there today towards the different accents and dialects that you have identified?

4 Many people argue that Standard English is 'only another dialect'. What do they mean by this? Do you agree?

5 If Standard English is simply one dialect among many, why do we use it – in speech and in writing – when we are being interviewed for a job, or writing an essay?

Introduction · as a class

Read together the extract from Act 3 of *Pygmalion* on **Worksheets 66a–b**. As you do so, think about the accent and dialect of the scene.

in pairs

In pairs, highlight the following on your worksheets in different colours:

- Examples of non-Standard English dialect (e.g. 'they done the old woman in').
- Examples of very polite and formal Standard English (e.g. 'Colonel Pickering, is it not?').
- Places where you think Liza reveals her Cockney accent, despite her attempts to conceal it.

Be prepared to feed back your ideas to the class.

Development · as a group

Read through the extract from Act 3 of *Pygmalion* again; this time you are going to analyse the dramatic features of the scene. As you read the playscript, therefore, think about how the characters are represented, and what aspects of the drama contribute to the humour of the scene.

Your teacher will divide you into five groups and allocate each group one of the following questions. Discuss your question, noting down the key points that are made and referring where relevant to the playscript, so that you can report them back to the class.

1 Shaw uses dialogue very skilfully to characterize Liza and the other players in this scene. What do we learn about the kind of people that they are? (Think about each one in turn.)

2 What are the main challenges facing the actress playing Liza in this scene? What advice would you give her?

3 Higgins speaks and behaves badly in lines 24–32 when he realizes that the Eynsford Hills have already met Liza (at Covent Garden, in Act 1; see starter). Why do you think Shaw has made him behave like this?

4 If you were the director, how would you make the most of the tension of this scene – that Higgins doesn't want Liza to be exposed?

5 What are the main elements that contribute to the humour of this scene?

Plenary

At the end of *Pygmalion* Liza breaks away from Higgins. Do you think learning Standard English was an important step on her road to independence? Write 'Yes, indeed' or 'Cam awf it!' on your whiteboard or a piece of paper and be prepared to give your reasons.

Dramatic irony in The Rivals

Aims

On these two pages you will:

- Analyse the impact of a scene from Sheridan's *The Rivals*, focusing on its use of dramatic irony.
- Rehearse different interpretations of the scene and compare their effect.
- Improvise a short dialogue to practise revealing the subtext of a character's speech.

Starter *in pairs*

We often don't say exactly what we think. As you will see when you analyse a scene from *The Rivals* later this lesson, actors often have to be able to show their real thoughts – the **subtext** that lies behind their spoken words.

Your teacher will give each pair a card, which will contain the opening line of a dialogue, together with the real thoughts of the speaker (**Worksheet 67**). Your task is to improvise a short dialogue (no more than two minutes) in which the speaker manages to show the audience something of his or her real thoughts, without actually saying them. You could think about:

- Tone
- Gesture
- Facial expression
- Pace/hesitation
- Choice of words.

Your teacher will ask some pairs to act out their dialogues. What methods have they used to reveal the subtext?

subtext a message which is not stated directly but hinted at in some way; also, an underlying theme in a piece of writing

Introduction *as a class*

Like Jane Austen (see pages 66–67), the playwright Richard Brinsley Sheridan wanted to poke fun at the manners and rules that governed 'polite' society in the 18th century. His play *The Rivals* is full of larger than life characters such as Mrs Malaprop and Captain Absolute. Mrs Malaprop's attempts to impress people by using long words – with disastrous effect – are not just a bit of fun: the writer is also making a point about snobs.

Read the extract from Act 3 scene 3 of *The Rivals* as a class (**Worksheets 68a–b**). The plot is a complex one, so make sure you read the synopsis first.

 in pairs

Sheridan was a master of **dramatic irony**: in this scene the audience knows that Captain Absolute is also 'Ensign Beverley' – the very author of the letter that he has to read out to Mrs Malaprop. She therefore becomes even more a figure of fun as she says things that are completely false (for example, 'ensign, whom none of us have seen' – yet she is looking at him) or ironically true (for example, 'perhaps you may know the writing' – of course he does: it is his own writing).

In pairs, highlight on the script all the places where dramatic irony is used in this way. Be prepared to discuss the lines you have highlighted and explain how they are effective.

dramatic irony the effect created in a play when the audience knows what is really going on but one or more of the characters does not

Development as a group

Sheridan's **comedies of manners** are often performed in an ostentatious or 'over the top' style, which emphasizes the mannerisms of the characters, the wit of the dialogue and the complex but racy nature of the plot.

Explore the best way of bringing out the wit, tension and humour in this scene by rehearsing it in two ways: one more ostentatious and one more realistic. Your teacher will divide you into groups of three and tell you which version your group is to rehearse. One member of each group should be the director. As you rehearse, think about the following:

- How the characters say their lines: exaggerated or deadpan?
- How much they use their bodies to move and gesture.
- How they interact with each other.
- How much they bring the audience in on the joke (what use do they make of the asides?).

Be prepared to present your version of the scene in front of the class.

Discuss the differences between the versions. Which are most successful and why?

comedy of manners a comedy which explores the way in which a particular social group behaves

Mrs Malaprop and Captain Absolute in The Rivals

Plenary

What is dramatic irony and what effect can it have in the theatre?

homework

For homework, write a short explanation of dramatic irony for Year 7 students, using two or three examples from Act 3 scene 3 of *The Rivals*.

! **Remember** to read your work through carefully and correct any mistakes. Have you written your explanation in a way that is appropriate for a Year 7 audience? Are your examples from the playscript well chosen, and referred to or quoted correctly? End with a brief comment telling your teacher how well you think you have done this piece of work.

Aims

On these two pages you will:

- Analyse the language, structure and characterization in a scene from Willy Russell's *Our Day Out*.
- Discuss how you would direct the scene, and annotate the playscript with notes for the actors.
- Identify the characteristics of Standard English that make it the dominant form of public communication.

Starter  as a class

In the extract from *Our Day Out* that you will be studying later this lesson, Carol says:

> 'Why can't I live in one of them nice white houses an' do the garden an' that?'

What parts of this sentence are in non-Standard English? What would they be in Standard English?

 as a group

The playwright was attempting to reproduce the speech of a schoolgirl from Liverpool, which is why he included these informal and dialect features. All of us speak English in our own individual way, with varying degrees of formality and with different dialects depending on our occupation, social background, racial origin, the region where we live and who we are with.

So why is Standard English taught in schools, especially in its written form? Because it is the dominant form of public communication. To explore this idea further, your teacher will give each group a set of cards (**Worksheet 69**) which list characteristics either of Standard English or of other dialects (non-Standard English). Your task is to group the cards under the correct heading and be prepared to explain your selection.

Introduction as a group

This lesson you are going to analyse a scene from a modern play, Willy Russell's *Our Day Out*. In the next two lessons you will improvise a scenario related to this scene and use it as the basis for a short scene of your own which you will write and perform.

Our Day Out describes how Mrs Kay's 'progress class' of 14-year-olds are taken for a day's coach trip to Conway Castle in Wales. The uptight and oppressive teacher Briggs joins the trip to keep an eye on the students' behaviour and tries to reduce the havoc that he fears they will cause. This scene proves to be the turning point in the play, when Briggs shows that he has a human side. It is also a turning point (literally) for the unhappy schoolgirl Carol, who is persuaded not to jump off the cliff. Read the scene together as a class (**Worksheets 70a–b**). Then discuss the following questions in groups:

1 Why does Carol threaten to jump off the cliff?

2 Where in the scene does she finally change her mind? Why?

3 Briggs tries several different ways to get Carol off the cliff (beginning by ordering her). What ways does he try, and how does this contribute to a deepening and softening of his character?

4 How does the playwright maintain tension throughout this scene?

5 Carol reaches out to Briggs at the end of the scene. How would you highlight this critical point if you were directing the scene?

6 Do you think this scene is effective? Give reasons for your views.

Be prepared to feed back your ideas, and to point to evidence in the playscript to support the points that you make.

Development as a group

One of the most important jobs that a director has is to advise the actors about how to deliver their lines, so that:

- The tone, pitch and pace is in line with their character
- Any subtext is suggested
- The scene is interpreted in a consistent and effective way.

Here are the kind of notes that a director might make on the opening lines of the scene you have been analysing:

a momentary hesitation as you see her, but it doesn't check your anger	BRIGGS	Carol Chandler! (*Briggs approaches. On seeing her he stops and stands a few yards off.*) Just come here.
		(*She turns and stares at him.*)
		Who gave you permission to come up here?
with disdain	CAROL	No-one. (*Turning she dismisses him.*)
getting angrier	BRIGGS	I'm talking to you, Carol Chandler.
		(*She continues to ignore his presence.*)
		Now just listen here, young lady ...
high-pitched, showing panic for the first time		(*As he goes to move towards her, she turns on him.*)
	CAROL	Don't you come near me!
each word separate and emphasized, as if trying to calm yourself as well as make your point	BRIGGS	(*taken aback, stopping*) Pardon!
	CAROL	I don't want you to come near me.
	BRIGGS	Well, in that case just get yourself moving and let's get down to the beach. *slightly embarrassed and confused – you're trying to be careless about it*

Your teacher will give each group a set of lines to annotate as if they were directing the scene. Discuss how you want to interpret your section to bring out its full dramatic potential, and record your ideas and instructions on the playscript.

Plenary

Some groups will be asked to present their interpretations, following the director's notes that they have made. What makes their interpretations effective?

Writing a script

Aims

On these two pages you will:

- Improvise a scene which resolves the tension between a parent and a teenager.
- Write a script for a scene based on the improvisation, which conveys tension and character.

Starter *as a group*

In the scene that you studied in the last lesson, a crisis brought out a significant change in both of the characters. A crisis was followed by **resolution**. This lesson you are going to work in groups to improvise a similar scenario, which will then act as the basis for a script for the scene.

Look at the scenario (right). In your group of five, decide who is going to play each role. You will all work out the bare bones of your improvisation together in advance, but the member of the group without an acting role will have the final say as director.

SCENARIO

A teenager is on the verge of leaving home. S/he is fed up with his/her father's anger and lack of understanding. S/he is struggling in a new school, expects to fail forthcoming exams, and has just been dumped by his/her boy/girlfriend. (The father doesn't know this.)
The father feels that he is losing touch with the teenager, but all he can do is to attack him/her. His relationship with **his wife** is also at crisis point – she has threatened to leave him – which adds to his anger and upset. (The teenager doesn't know this.)
The teenager's brother/sister is bewildered by the tension in the household but feels powerless to do anything about it.
An incident provokes a major crisis, as a result of which there is some kind of resolution.

Characters

- Father
- Teenager
- Mother
- Brother/sister

resolution the resolving of the crisis, tension or other problem in a scene

Introduction *as a group*

To explore the possibilities of this scenario, try out different opening lines and see where they lead. You may like to start with these opening lines from the father:

or these opening lines from the teenager:

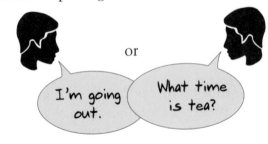

I'm going out.

What time is tea?

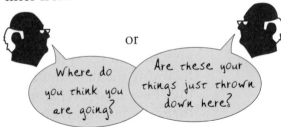

or

Where do you think you are going?

Are these your things just thrown down here?

Try different ways of bringing your scenario to a crisis, and different ways in which the situation is resolved. Think about the following questions as you try out your improvisation:

- What incident will provoke the crisis that is the focus of your scene?
- How will this crisis lead to a resolution?
- What sort of resolution will it be – a change of action or character, or a new understanding or outlook?
- How will you build up the tension?
- Could you use dramatic irony to increase the tension and impact of the scene?
- How will the dialogue bring out the characters?
- What role will the two minor characters play (mother and brother/ sister)? For example, will their actions and/or character reflect on or contrast with the main action?
- What other dramatic techniques will you use?
- How can you end the scene in the most effective way?

Use the planning frame on **Worksheet 71** to help you plan your most effective improvisation. Then act it out.

Development *as a group*

Your task now is to write a script for the scene, basing it on the improvisation that worked the best. Follow these steps:

First discuss whether your improvisation could be improved in any way. Decide what key changes you need to make to improve it, if any. Try not to make a completely new plan, but to adapt the plan that you have made on **Worksheet 71**.

Draft your group's script. Each member of the group should concentrate on developing their own character's part within the scene. The director, who will supply the stage directions, will have the final say on how the scene is shaped, both in detail and as a whole.

Read the first draft of your script aloud and see if it works. Think about how to present the crisis and resolution, and about movement and gesture, as well as what is said and how it is said. As you discuss the script, annotate your copy with notes about how it could be improved.

Using the annotated copy of the script to help you, amend the script to produce a final draft.

Plenary

What crisis has your group constructed, and how is it resolved?

homework

Familiarize yourself with your part in the script for homework, as next lesson you will be performing the script. The director should annotate their copy of the script so that they can advise the actors about how to deliver their lines, as you did for the scene from *Our Day Out* (see page 91 above).

Evaluating the performances

Aims

On these two pages you will:

- Perform the scene that you have scripted and evaluate the performances of other groups, commenting on the acting, the writing and the direction.
- Evaluate your contributions to all the drama activities in which you have played a part this year.

Starter *as a class*

You are going to warm up for the performances this lesson by playing 'In the manner of the word'. Your teacher will ask for a volunteer to leave the room. When he or she is out of earshot, you should all agree on an adverb, such as 'angrily' or 'carelessly', and form a large circle.

When the volunteer comes back into the room he or she should enter the circle and ask you to perform a certain action 'in the manner of the word'. Anything can be chosen as the action:

- Washing the car
- Addressing a meeting
- Putting on your shoes.

Really get into the action and express yourself 'in the manner of the word' – can the volunteer guess what the adverb is?

Now try it again with further volunteers – each time there should be a different adverb chosen and a different activity to perform it to.

Introduction *as a group*

You have got 15 minutes in which to rehearse the scene that you scripted in the last lesson. The director should make sure that the actors' speech, movements and gestures all contribute to the desired interpretation of the scene. In particular, remember:

- To grab the audience's attention with the opening.
- To pace the scene so that you build up the tension and then release it in the resolution.
- To make use of the minor characters to add depth and meaning to the main relationship.
- To use gesture, facial expression and movement as well as words and silence.
- To think about tone and expression when delivering your lines.
- To end the scene in an effective and memorable way.

Can you also make use of dramatic irony?

Development as a class

Now perform your playscript to the class. Evaluate the performances of the other groups by filling in the grid on **Worksheet 72**. (Keep this worksheet, as you will need to refer to it when you write a review of one of the performances in the next lesson.)

Discuss what made the winning group's performance the most popular. Did the writing, the direction and the acting all contribute equally to its success?

Plenary

Think back over all the drama activities in which you have played a part this year, and evaluate your strengths and weaknesses using **Worksheet 73**. Think of three skills and/or techniques that you have developed, and set yourself three targets to improve your performance.

Acting and working in role	Yes	Sometimes	No
Am I willing to adopt a variety of roles?			
Do I sustain and deepen the roles that I adopt?			
Do I interact effectively with the other characters?			

Looking at listings

Aims

On these two pages you will:

- Analyse the structure and style of a listings entry, using terms that describe language.
- Write a listings entry of a performance that you have seen, using the appropriate degree of formality.
- Identify different degrees of formality in language, and the contexts for which they are appropriate.

Starter  as a group

As you know, there are many different degrees of formality in the language that we speak and write. For example:

- **Slang** – deliberately non-Standard English, often used to show that one belongs to a certain group.
- **Colloquial language** – conversational language, often using contractions, slang and dialect.
- **Informal language** – loosely structured, casual language which sometimes ignores grammatical rules and can include slang and colloquialisms.
- **Formal language** – which in vocabulary, structure, grammar and spelling follows the rules of Standard English.

If you listed these different levels on a scale ranging from the most informal to the most formal your scale would look something like this:

Each group will be given 16 words or phrases, together with the headings Slang, Colloquial, Informal and Formal (**Worksheet 74**). Your task is to group the words under what you think is the most appropriate heading.

 as a class

Compare your choices with those of the other groups. Did you agree?

Each type of language is appropriate to different forms of writing and speaking. Name a situation in which each type of language is appropriate.

Introduction as a class

This lesson and next you will be analysing the style and content of two very different kinds of theatre review, and writing your own reviews in a similar style.

First, read the **listings** on page 97 as a class. These listings tell the reader what performances are on, and where and when they are on, but do they do any more than this? Is there anything in the text to persuade (or dissuade) you from going to see the performances?

in pairs

Your teacher will show you how to analyse the vocabulary, structure, grammar and style of the first entry (**Worksheet 75**). Your job, in pairs,

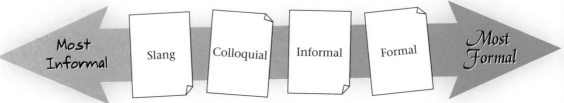

Most Informal — Slang — Colloquial — Informal — Formal — *Most Formal*

is to annotate and highlight the text of the second entry in a similar way. Be prepared to present your analysis to the class, using the appropriate terms to describe the language and structure.

> **listings** a list of concerts, films and other events printed in a newspaper or magazine

Performance

THE RIVALS
Salisbury Playhouse
Thursday September 6–Saturday 29 at 8pm
Sheridan's top quipping Restoration comedy – all mistaken identity and improbable outcomes from the scribbler of School for Scandal. Set in Georgian Bath and featuring the legendary word-mangler Mrs Malaprop.

THE REAL THING
Bristol Old Vic
Friday September 7–Saturday 29 at 7.30pm
Tom Stoppard honed his gifts for writing at Bristol's very own Evening Post, and his complex prose returns to the city with this revival of his bittersweet comedy about the merging of professional and personal lives for playwright Henry (Neil Pearson from telly's Drop the Dead Donkey). Quality board-treaders Marsha Fitzalan (from The New Statesman) and Geraldine Alexander (who's not really a TV sort of person) complete the line up.

Development *on your own*

Now it's your turn to write a similar listings entry for one of the performances that you watched last lesson. Imagine that it is to be included in your school magazine. It should be only one or two sentences long. Consider the following questions before you write your entry:

- What information about the plot, the performance and the actors do you want to include?
- How will you write the entry in the most concise way to include as much as you can in a short space?
- How can you add humour through your use of informal or colloquial language?
- Will you suggest what you think about the play or the acting through your use of language?
- Will you give personal details about the directors and actors to add sparkle to the entry and help the readers identify them?
- What title are you going to give to the performance?

Use your evaluation sheet from the last lesson to help you (**Worksheet 72**), and jot down your thoughts on **Worksheet 76** before writing the entry at the bottom of the worksheet.

Plenary

Your teacher will ask some of you to read out your listings entries. Which are the most effective and why? Is the formality of the language and style appropriate to their purpose and audience?

Reviewing a review

Aims

On these two pages you will:

- Analyse the content, language and structure of a broadsheet theatre review.
- Compose a review of your own, writing in Standard English with the degree of formality suited to its audience and purpose.
- Compare this review with the listings entry that you wrote last lesson.
- Explain how punctuation is used to clarify and emphasize meaning.

Starter  as a class

Why do we use punctuation when we write?

 in pairs

Look carefully at the passage below. In pairs, identify each punctuation mark and make sure you can explain why the writer has included it. Be prepared to feed back to the class.

> The modern punctuation system is extremely wide-ranging, including such features as spaces, indentation, the use of capitals, and a wide range of non-alphabetic graphic cues (such as asterisks and footnote numerals), as well as the traditional 'marks'. Some features identify large units of writing, such as paragraphs and sections; some identify small units, such as words or word parts; some identify units of intermediate size or complexity, such as sentences, clauses, and phrases. Most marks are features that separate – showing the boundaries between grammatical constructions.

Introduction as a group

Newspapers and magazines often include extended theatre reviews as well as listings. These reviews provide a fuller analysis of the production, and they are written in a style that reflects that of the newspaper in which they are published. A professional reviewer for a broadsheet newspaper will try hard to make his or her review a stylish piece of writing, which is intended not only to provide facts and opinions about the production but also to be enjoyed as a small literary essay in its own right.

George Bernard Shaw's *Pygmalion* was turned into the highly successful musical comedy *My Fair Lady* in 1956. Read the review of the National Theatre's 2001 production of *My Fair Lady* on **Worksheet 77**. Then, in groups, discuss the following questions:

1 Which parts of the review tell you about the acting?

2 Which parts of the review tell you about the production and direction?

3 Identify four descriptive adjectives and four powerful verbs that are particularly imaginative or effective, and explain why the writer has used them.

4 Many of the sentences are complex, containing several subordinate clauses. Identify some sentences that are shorter and explain why the writer has included them.

5 The review is written in Standard English, but occasionally an informal word or phrase is used (for example, 'gives Nunn's production a satirical shot in the vitals'). Why has the writer done this?

6 Why has the reviewer ended with the sentence 'Fairly magical, indeed'? Is this an effective ending?

Be prepared to feed back your ideas to the class.

Development *on your own*

Last lesson you wrote a short listings entry on one of the performances that you watched. Now it's time to think about that performance again, and this time write a longer review (about four paragraphs). Imagine that it is to be submitted to an upmarket local newspaper.

- Unlike the review of *My Fair Lady*, you cannot assume that your readers know the play. Part of the review, therefore, should be devoted to explaining what the performance is about, and commenting on the script.

- You should also comment on the acting and direction, using the notes that you made on your evaluation grid to help you (**Worksheet 72**).

- You may decide to devote one paragraph to each of these topics. Alternatively you may wish to use a more complex structure, weaving your comments on all these aspects of the production together.

- Either way, try to use imaginative verbs and adjectives to grab the interest of the reader, and give the piece an effective ending.

> **!** *Remember* to read your work carefully. Have you used Standard English (except where you want to make a particular point) and an appropriate degree of formality? Have you used punctuation to clarify and emphasize meaning? Improve your review if necessary and write a brief comment on how well you think you have completed the task.

Plenary

Write on your whiteboard or a piece of paper three key ways in which the style or structure of your review differs from that of the listings entry that you wrote last lesson.

Martine McCutcheon as Eliza and Mark Umbers as Freddy in My Fair Lady

The celebrity interview

Aims

On these two pages you will:

- Analyse the structure and style of a celebrity interview in a magazine.
- Interview each other and write it up as an article in a similar style, focusing on the appropriate formality of language and integrating speech effectively.
- Discuss how to increase the speed and accuracy of your note-taking.

Starter *as a class*

1. What do the following symbols mean? How could these symbols be used to increase the speed and accuracy of your note-taking?

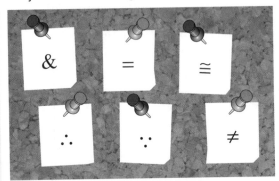

2. Now look at the following message:

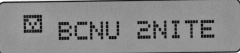

What other abbreviations do you use when you text your friends? Do any of you use these abbreviations in your note-taking? Think about how you text and e-mail your friends, and share with the class the ways in which you speed up your messages. Write these abbreviations in your schoolbook and use them when you have to take notes.

Introduction *as a group*

Many interviews in newspapers and magazines focus on the lives of the rich and famous. Some interviews are intended to glamorize the private life and relationships of the celebrity; their main purpose is to entertain the reader. Others probe more deeply into issues related to the celebrity's career, their ideas or their background.

Read the interview with Victoria Beckham which appeared in the *Daily Mirror* (**Worksheet 78**). Your teacher will divide you into five groups and allocate each group one of the following questions. Discuss your question, noting down the key points that are made and referring where relevant to the article, so that you can report back your ideas to the class.

1. What do you learn from this interview about Victoria Beckham's a) appearance, b) personality, c) attitude to life, d) history?

2. What reason is given for the interview and where is this given? What is the purpose of the first four paragraphs? Is this an effective opening?

3. How much of the article is direct quotation and how much is the interviewer's description or comments? The interviewer, Tony Parsons, does not usually quote his questions directly. What methods does he use to suggest his questions and keep the dialogue going?

4 Do we learn anything about Tony Parsons from this article? What do you think is his attitude to Victoria Beckham?

5 How formal is the language of this interview? Is there any difference in register between the words of the interviewer and those of the interviewee? Is the level of formality appropriate to the context and audience of this piece?

Victoria Beckham

Development *in pairs*

You are a celebrity, and you are going to be interviewed for five minutes by your partner for an article in *Cool* magazine, which is aimed at young teenagers. The article is to focus on your home life, and include reference to your friendships (past and present) and your personality.

1 First of all spend a minute or two getting in role – you are a world-famous celebrity (a singer? a footballer? an actor?) with a very ordinary home life. Then be prepared to be as forthcoming and helpful as possible when you answer your interviewer's questions.

2 Now it's your turn to interview your partner. Remember the techniques that you discussed and used on pages 80–81, especially asking questions to draw out further information from your interviewee. Remember also to use the techniques you discussed in the starter activity to increase the speed and accuracy of your note-taking. Try to note down exactly the words of your interviewee, as you will be quoting some of these in your article, and make a note also of the questions that you asked.

on your own

Now draft your article. Before you begin, jot down your thoughts on the structure and style of your interview on **Worksheet 79**.

Plenary

Your teacher will ask some of you to read out the opening paragraphs of your draft celebrity interview. Are they effective openings? Is the style appropriate for an article in *Cool* magazine?

homework

Write a final draft of your celebrity interview for homework.

> **!** **Remember** to read through your work carefully. Have you integrated speech into the article in an effective way? Is the formality of your writing appropriate for the context and audience? Improve your interview if necessary and write a brief comment on how well you think you completed the task.

Analysing an analysis

Aims

On these two pages you will:

- Analyse an analysis article from a newspaper, focusing on its structure and language and how it explains the connection between ideas.
- Rewrite information that is in bullet form as a cohesive paragraph of text, explaining the connection between ideas.

Starter

This lesson you will be looking in detail at another type of newspaper and magazine article, one that attempts to analyse a controversial or complex topic in a balanced way, taking account of a range of evidence and opinions. Sometimes such an article is described simply as 'Analysis'.

When you are analysing a complex issue, it is important that your paragraphs are cohesive: the connection between the ideas should be clear so that the reader can follow the meaning. To help you practise this, try the activity on **Worksheet 80**, which asks you to compose an effective and cohesive paragraph about sharks.

Introduction in pairs

Read the newspaper article on fox hunting on page 103 as a class. This article has two purposes, as it combines:

- News and explanation about a topical issue (the vote in Parliament on hunting)
- Analysis of the underlying issues of the rights and wrongs of fox hunting, backed up by the opinions of the interested parties.

How does the writer structure his article so that it does both of these things in a short space? In pairs, try the activity on **Worksheet 81**.

Development as a group

Now read the article again in groups and discuss the following questions:

1 How formal is the language? Is this appropriate to the content, purpose and audience of the article?

2 Why has the writer decided in the main article to summarize the opinions of the two sides rather than quote them directly?

3 Identify the main place where there are direct quotations. Why has the writer chosen to display them in this way?

4 How fair has the writer been in explaining the views of each side? Can you tell what the writer's own views are on this issue?

5 How much evidence has the writer given to back up the views of each side?

6 Why does the article end by mentioning Prince Charles? Is this an effective ending?

Be prepared to feed back your ideas to the class.

Plenary

Write down on your whiteboard, or on a piece of paper, three features that make an effective 'analysis' article in a newspaper or magazine.

Should there be a ban on hunting?

by Jerome Monahan

A vote by MPs tomorrow could bring a ban on using dogs to hunt foxes, deer, hare and mink a big step closer. For the League Against Cruel Sports, this would mean the end of a 76-year campaign. For fans of field sports, this would threaten centuries-old countryside traditions.

Surveys suggest most people in Britain oppose blood sports. But, say hunting enthusiasts, it is unfair for city people to judge lifestyles they do not understand, and unjust for Parliament to ban them. But it looks as if this is what Parliament will do tomorrow when MPs are given the freedom to vote how they like, "according to conscience". Normally an MP is expected to support the views of the political party they belong to.

MPs will have to opt for one of three courses of action, instead of the usual yes/no decision. They will be able to vote for a complete ban, for strict outside regulation of hunting with dogs, or for a voluntary system in which hunting people would supervise their own activities.

Even if the vote goes against hunting, huntsmen in England and Wales will not be hanging up their red coats just yet. The same three choices have to be debated in the House of Lords, and it is possible that they will reverse the MPs' decision. The government can overturn the Lords' vote but they may not have time to do so before the next General Election, expected to be in May. The laws may change sooner in Scotland because the Scottish Parliament, which is also discussing these issues, does not have a House of Lords. Hunting deer with dogs is already illegal in Scotland.

The present hunting bill follows a major independent inquiry into hunting, the Burns Report, published last June. It agreed that the welfare of foxes was "seriously <u>compromised</u>"[1] by being chased and caught by hounds.

Supporters of hunting argue that hunting foxes is just as humane as the other methods used to kill them. Their opponents say that death for foxes and hares does not come with a single bite from the first dog, but while they are being torn to pieces by the pack. They also argue that the stresses animals suffer when chased can kill them – even if they escape.

> **What they said …**
>
> *'The English country gentleman galloping after a fox – the unspeakable in pursuit of the uneatable.'*
> **Oscar Wilde**
>
> *'The issue of hunting has become a litmus test of the government's commitment to a society of tolerance and democracy.'*
> **Sam Butler, Chairman, Countryside Alliance**
>
> *'I believe that hunting with dogs is a barbaric practice that in no way can be justified as sport.'*
> **Sir Paul McCartney**

The Burns Report estimated that up to 8,000 jobs could be lost if hunting was banned and there is already huge unemployment in rural areas.

Then there are the moral arguments. Should people take pleasure in killing animals? Then again, would people care so much if rats were the quarry?

If the issue features in an election, it may be to the advantage of the Labour Party, which does well when young people vote. Few subjects get young voters involved as much as hunting. A ban could also be positive for the health of Prince Charles, who recently broke a bone in his shoulder by falling from his horse while fox-hunting.

1 *affected*

Analysis: Is slang cool?

Aims

On these two pages you will:

- Write your own analysis article on slang, taking into account a range of evidence and opinions and focusing on the formality of your language, paragraph cohesion and integrating quotations effectively.
- Explore in more detail the characteristics of slang and discuss different attitudes towards it.

Starter *as a class*

1 What exactly is slang? Discuss this with your partner and try to come up with an agreed definition of the word 'slang', before feeding back your ideas to the class.

2 Read together the article from the *English Standard* below. Why was the government report so controversial?

ENGLISH STANDARD 31 June 2002

Teachers' leaders in a stew over report *by our literacy correspondent*

Teachers' leaders were up in arms over the publication yesterday of a government report which suggested that slang and other informal language should be just as acceptable as Standard English in written exams, so as not to discriminate against 'natural forms of expression'. The report, commissioned by the Department of Education and Training, is itself written in unusually informal language, and even contains slang terms such as 'aggro' and 'barmy'. The government was unavailable for comment yesterday, but the Education Secretary, S. L. Morris, was said to be 'up a gumtree' by the publication of the report.

Introduction *as a group*

This lesson you are going to write your own analysis of a controversial issue – slang – to be published in a broadsheet newspaper aimed at young teenagers. The article has been commissioned by the *English Standard* newspaper as a follow-up to the news item that you have just read.

Discuss in groups what you already know about slang:

- What is the definition of slang? (Think back to the starter activity, left.)
- What words or phrases are classified as 'slang'? (Think back to the starter on page 96 and look at the extract from a dictionary of slang on page 105.)
- What are the functions and characteristics of non-Standard English? (Think back to the starter on page 90.)
- When is it appropriate to use slang? (Think back to the starter, left, and the starter on page 96.)

Jot down your ideas on your brainstorming sheet (**Worksheet 82**). Then read the information and views about slang on **Worksheet 83** together, and discuss the different views expressed.

Be prepared to feed back to the class.

Development on your own

Your article should be called 'Analysis: Is slang cool?' It should be no longer than six paragraphs. Before you begin, read the panel below.

How to write a cool 'analysis' article on slang

- State the main issue at the start, for example 'When is it appropriate to use slang?', and link it in with the news item to give the article topical relevance.

- Briefly explain what slang is and what its functions and characteristics are.

- Explain the opinions of people who hold different views on this issue. The article must be a *balanced* analysis of the issue: you should not reveal your own views.

- Quote the actual words of some of the people who hold strong or interesting views on the issue, and/or report their words using indirect speech.

- Give examples of slang words and phrases where relevant.

- Write in cohesive paragraphs to make the connection between your ideas clear.

- End in an effective and entertaining way.

Now draft your article, using your notes on **Worksheet 82** and the evidence and opinions on **Worksheet 83** to help you.

 in pairs

Swap your draft with a partner's and read each other's draft carefully, bearing in mind the points that must be covered. In turn, discuss how each draft could be improved. Annotate your drafts with suggestions for improvement.

Plenary

Your teacher will ask some of you to read the opening paragraphs of your article. Do they state the issue clearly and effectively, and link it in with the news item?

homework

Compose a final draft of your analysis for homework.

> **!** **Remember** to read your work carefully. Have you written in Standard English, with a formality appropriate to the purpose and audience of the article? Are your paragraphs cohesive, explaining clearly the connection between ideas? Have you worked quotations and evidence into your article effectively?
>
> Make any changes if necessary, and write a brief comment explaining why you think this final version is an improvement on your first draft.

abdabs *Noun*. Terror, the frights, nerves. Often heard as *the screaming abdabs*. [1940s]

Abysinnia! *Exclam*. A jocular and intentional mispronunciation of 'I'll be seeing you!'

accidentally-on-purpose *Phrs*. Seemingly accidental but with veiled malice or harm.

ace (!) *Adj*. Excellent, wonderful.
Exclam. Excellent!

ackers *Noun*. Money. From the Egyptian *akka*.

action man *Noun*. A man who participates in macho activities.

Adam and Eve *Verb*. Believe. Cockney rhyming slang. E.g. 'I don't Adam and Eve it, it's not true!'

aerated *Adj*. Over-excited. Becoming obsolete, although still heard used by older generations. Often mispronounced as *aeriated*.

aggro *Noun*. Aggressive troublemaking, violence, aggression. Abb. of aggravation.

Reviewing what's been learnt

In this section you have analysed the style, structure and dramatic impact of three different plays. You have thought in detail about how effective dramatic irony can be on the stage. You have also considered what the playwright, the actors and the director each bring to make a play a successful dramatic experience, and developed your skills in each of these areas, especially in improvising a scenario and then devising a script to present it.

In the second half of the section you have extended your knowledge and understanding of journalism by analysing different kinds of newspaper and magazine articles. You have reviewed your own dramatic performances, interviewed your partner for a magazine and composed an in-depth analysis of the nature and purpose of slang.

Throughout the section you have explored different attitudes to the English language – spoken and written, Standard and non-Standard, formal and informal – and you should now be clear where each kind of language is appropriate and why Standard English is the dominant form of public communication.

Now it's time to think about what things you have learnt from this section and list the key points in your exercise book, using the sentence starters (right) to help you.

The key things I have learnt about writing playscripts in this section are ...

The key things I have learnt about newspaper and magazine articles are ...

I now understand more about ...

When presenting ideas, I now know ...

Some of the vocabulary I now feel more confident about using is ...

The things I found most difficult were ...

The things I think I did best were ...

I now feel more confident about ...

My targets to improve my work are:
(include reading, writing, speaking and listening)
-
-
-
-
-
-

Plan, draft, present

Introduction

Human beings have used poetry to express their hopes, fears and feelings for thousands of years. In this section you will focus on poetry written in the 20th century, ranging from the sonnet with its strict form and traditions, to free verse whose only rule is to reject all the rules. You will look at how different poets have been inspired by art as well as by a range of powerful human emotions, and you will analyse the different ingredients that poets have used to make their work effective. You will experiment with creating your own poetry within these varied traditions and decide how best to lay out one of these poems to maximize its effect.

You will use your increasing powers of analysis to compare a variety of poems and develop your ability to plan and write a well-expressed essay in formal English and under timed conditions. Then you will review your writing skills, not just for formal essays but for the wide range of writing activities that you will be attempting in this section.

Finally, you will work on problem solving, planning in a group the logistics of how to organize a series of presentations. And throughout all these activities you will record, evaluate and seek to develop your speaking and listening skills, setting targets for future improvement.

Key aims

In this section you will:

- Understand more about some of the great poems written in the last century and the hopes and fears that inspired them, and use some of their ideas to create your own poems.

- Develop your skills at analysing poetry and writing about it formally in a coherent, well-expressed essay, as well as being able to take part in a group presentation about the poem you liked best.

WENDY COPE

Serious Concerns

Wishing your life away

Aims

On these two pages you will:

- Analyse what makes 'Rising Five' an effective poem.
- Think about how the form of a poem can contribute to its meaning.
- Write your own poem about age.

Starter

Without speaking to anyone else, concentrate on what you think is the perfect age – the age you would like to be. Think of the key reasons for your choice. When requested, secretly write this age in large numbers on your whiteboard or a piece of paper.

At a signal from your teacher hold up your chosen age. Look round the room and see if most people in the class have selected a similar age. Be prepared to discuss the reasons for people's choices.

Introduction as a class

Listen carefully while your teacher reads you Norman Nicholson's poem 'Rising Five' (page 109) and think about the following questions. Once you've heard the poem, you will have a chance to discuss these questions with a partner before joining the class discussion.

1 What is the poet trying to say?
2 What difference does the layout of the poem make to its meaning?
3 What ingredients help make this poem effective? (Use the noticeboard on **Worksheet 84** to help you – it is repeated below.)
4 Which lines do you find the most effective?

Writer's purpose:
Theme:
Narrative perspective:
autobiographical: autobiographical style – persona: monologue: third person, etc.
Tone: formal, informal, serious, sad, comic, mocking, ironic, etc.
Form: overall structure: line structure: rhythm: rhyme
Style:

- choice of vocabulary – (simple, elaborate, varied)
- word order (diction)
- imagery and figurative language (including simile, metaphor, personification)
- sound effects (repetition, alliteration, assonance, onomatopoeia)

Rising Five

'I'm rising five,' he said.
'Not four,' and little coils of hair
Un-clicked themselves upon his head.
His spectacles, brimful of eyes to stare
At me and the meadow, reflected cones of light
Above his toffee-buckled cheeks. He'd been alive
Fifty-six months or perhaps a week more:
                  not four,

But rising five.

Around him in the field the cells of spring
Bubbled and doubled; buds unbuttoned; shoot
And stem shook out the creases from their frills,
And every tree was swilled with green.
It was the season after blossoming,
Before the forming of the fruit:
             not May,

But rising June.
              And in the sky
The dust dissected the <u>tangential</u>[1] light:
          not day,

But rising night;
       not now,
But rising soon.

The new buds push the old leaves from the bough.
We drop our youth behind us like a boy
Throwing away his toffee-wrappers. We never see
  the flower,
But only the fruit in the flower; never the fruit,
But only the rot in the fruit. We look for the
  marriage bed
In the baby's cradle, we look for the grave
  in the bed:
          not living,
But rising dead.

Norman Nicholson

Norman Nicholson (1914–1987) lived all his life in Millom, a steel town in Cumbria. His poems focus on his local area and his religious beliefs.

Development *on your own*

The perfect age? Write your own poem, in any form that you like, about the age you would like to be. If you have chosen an age older than your present age, you may want to include what your feelings may be when you reach that age. When you reach that age, do you think you will want to be a different age after all? You may like to include this thought in your poem.

Plenary

What have your discussions about the perfect age suggested about human beings?

Is poetry a good medium to express these sorts of ideas?

slanting

Sonnet form

Aims

On these two pages you will:

- Read two sonnets and analyse sonnet form, thinking about the relationship between form and meaning.
- Write a poem in sonnet form, selecting the degree of formality appropriate to your chosen theme.

Starter  as a group

Listen carefully while your teacher reads you one of Shakespeare's sonnets, then discuss the following questions, using the footnotes to help you.

1 If you hadn't already been told that this is a sonnet, how could you tell?

2 What do you think Shakespeare is trying to say?

3 Which lines do you think are the wittiest?

Be prepared to feed your ideas back to the class.

> **iambic pentameter** a verse line consisting of five iambs, or metrical feet, each having a short syllable followed by a long syllable

What is a sonnet?

The sonnet is a verse form consisting of 14 lines of **iambic pentameter**. This means there are ten syllables to a line, with the first syllable unstressed and the second stressed throughout, as in the example below:

When my love swears that she is made of truth.

The rhymes are arranged according to a fixed order. The Italians favoured eight lines followed by six. The English favoured three four-line sections ending with a rhyming couplet, as in the example below.

Sonnet 138

When my love swears that she is made of <u>truth</u>,[1]
I do believe her though I know she lies,
That she might think me some untutored youth,
Unlearned in the world's false subtleties.
Thus vainly thinking that she thinks me young,
Although she knows my days are past the best,
<u>Simply</u>[2] I <u>credit</u>[3] her false-speaking tongue;
On both sides thus is simple truth suppressed.
But wherefore says she not she is <u>unjust</u>?[4]
And wherefore say not I that I am old?
O, love's best <u>habit</u>[5] is in <u>seeming trust</u>,[6]
And age in love loves not to have years <u>told</u>.[7]
   Therefore I <u>lie with</u>[8] her, and she with me,
   And in our faults by lies we flattered be.

William Shakespeare

[1] *(a) honesty (b) fidelity*
[2] *(a) foolishly (b) pretending to be simple*
[3] *believe*
[4] *unfaithful*
[5] *appearance*
[6] *the appearance of truth*
[7] *counted*
[8] *(a) lie to (b) sleep with*

Introduction *as a class*

Ever since Shakespeare's time, people have been writing sonnets in English – most of which are about love. As you can see in the example you have been discussing, form, rhythm and rhyme are all very important to a sonnet.

Here is a sonnet (right) by the contemporary poet Wendy Cope. The problem is that her sonnet has not been laid out in the correct line form. Your teacher will give you a copy of this sonnet in strips (**Worksheet 85**). Your task is to cut these strips up and sort them out so that the sonnet is laid out correctly. (She has used exactly the same rhyme scheme as Shakespeare.)

When you have constructed the sonnet, decide whether it is effective and which lines you like best. Be prepared to feed your ideas back to the class.

Development *on your own*

Now it's your turn to see if you can write a sonnet. Use your whiteboards or spare paper to draft your ideas. You may find it useful to use Wendy Cope's poem as a template, using the idea of what you could be remembered for as your theme, beginning with the phrase:

Not only ...

and ending with the rhymes:

... forgotten

... rotten.

Or you may decide to begin and end in your own way.

Not only marble but the plastic toys from cornflake packets will outlive this rhyme: I can't immortalise you, love – our joys will lie unnoticed in the vault of time. When Mrs Thatcher[1] has been cast in bronze and her administration is a page in some O-level[2] text-book, when the dons[3] have analysed the story of our age, when travel firms sell tours of outer space and aeroplanes take off without a sound and Tulse Hill[4] has become a trendy place and Upper Norwood's[5] on the underground, your beauty and my name will be forgotten – my love is true but all my verse is rotten.

Wendy Cope

[1] *Conservative Prime Minister, 1979–1990*
[2] *exam system prior to GCSEs*
[3] *university teachers, especially at Oxford or Cambridge*
[4,5] *south London suburbs beyond the reach of the Victoria Line*

Wendy Cope was born in Kent in 1945 and went to Oxford University. She is well known for witty, artful and subversive poems, many of which are parodies. Her first book of poems, *Making Cocoa for Kingsley Amis*, went straight into the best-seller lists.

Plenary

What makes sonnets potentially very effective?

What makes them hard to write?

homework

See if you can complete your sonnet to your satisfaction for homework.

! ***Remember*** to check that you have got ten syllables to every line and that the stress moves from unstressed to stressed throughout. When it's as good as you can get it, give your sonnet a final check through, making certain that it is laid out correctly. Write a brief comment on how successful you think your sonnet is.

Poems don't have to rhyme

Aims

On these two pages you will:

● Think about how form contributes to meaning and write a poem in free verse form.

● Reflect on your ability both as a speaker and a listener in a range of contexts and identify targets for improvement.

● Use grids to evaluate, record and develop your speaking and listening skills.

Starter *on your own*

The work that you are doing on poems throughout this section is also an opportunity for you to develop and evaluate your speaking and listening skills. Read the 'Speaking and listening challenge' box below and follow the instructions given there.

The Speaking and Listening Challenge

You will be listening to lots of different poems in this section and discussing your responses. This will involve you listening carefully to their sound effects, followed by group and class discussion, as well as close analysis of the poems. Later you will be discussing how different poets have dealt with similar topics and how best to organize an essay to compare and contrast their approaches. At the end of the section your challenge will be to organize the class into groups so that everyone can present the poems they enjoyed most.

To help you with this, you are going to analyse your strengths as a speaker and a listener, draw up some targets and keep a running record of how you are managing to meet these targets throughout the section.

Use the grid on **Worksheet 86** to help you analyse your strengths and weaknesses. Then set yourself at least two speaking and two listening targets for this section of work, which you should write on the back of the worksheet.

Introduction *as a class*

As you know, poems don't have to rhyme. After the First World War (1914–1918) there was a tendency for artists to reject tradition. This rebellion became known as Modernism. One of the leading poets of the American Modernist movement was William Carlos Williams who rejected formal rhythmic patterns and wrote in **free verse**. Listen to the sound of William Carlos Williams' poem 'This Is Just to Say' (page 113) and decide what makes it effective. Be prepared to discuss this with a partner and feed your ideas back to the class.

> **free verse** verse that has neither rhyme nor a regular rhythm

on your own

Use Williams' title 'This Is Just to Say' to write your own short poem about small things that you have done that perhaps you shouldn't have done and which deep down inside you probably don't actually regret. Experiment with writing in a similar line pattern to Williams'.

This Is Just to Say

I have eaten
the plums
that were
in the icebox

and which
you were probably
saving
for breakfast

Forgive me
they were delicious
so sweet
and so cold

William Carlos Williams

William Carlos Williams (1883–1963), poet and novelist, was a doctor in Paterson, near New York. He was the leader of an influential strand of American Modernism, adopting the approach 'No ideas but in things'. His apparently simple free-verse poems focus on immediate physical detail.

Development — as a class

Now listen carefully as your teacher reads you another poem by William Carlos Williams, 'The Red Wheelbarrow'.

Would it have been so effective if it had been written down like prose?

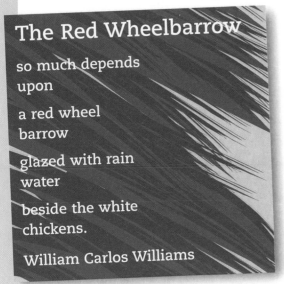

The Red Wheelbarrow

so much depends
upon

a red wheel
barrow

glazed with rain
water

beside the white
chickens.

William Carlos Williams

on your own

Taking Williams' opening phrase, 'So much depends', try writing your own poem using a similar line pattern. Write more than one poem if you have time.

as a group

Look at the poems that people within your group have written and decide which ones are the most effective. Be prepared to present these to the class.

Plenary

Listen as the poems are presented. Which ones do you think are the most effective, and why?

The Speaking and Listening Challenge

Fill in the first section of your speaking and listening record (**Worksheet 87a**).

Playing with syntax

On these two pages you will:

- Think about how the form of a poem, and the presentational devices it uses, contribute to its meaning.
- Review and use terms that are useful for analysing language.

Starter as a group

Look at the following short poem by Benjamin Zephaniah.

1 What do you think poetic licence means?

2 What presentational devices has the poet used, and how do these contribute to the poem's meaning?

Be prepared to feed back your ideas to the class.

According to my Mood

I have *poetic* **licence**, i wri**T**e th**E** way i wa**Nt**.

i *drop* my **full stops** when *i* like...

MY CAPITAL Lete**R**s go where *i* li**KE**,

i **order** from **MY** PeN, i verse **the way** i like

(**i do** *my spelling write*)

According to My **MO**od.

i **HA**ve **P**oetic **licence**,

i put my **commers** where **i** like,, ((**O**).

(((**my** brackets *are* **write**((

ı REPEAT **WH**en i lik**E**.

i can't **go** rong.

i *look* and **i.e.**

I**t**'s **rite.**

ı**ı** REPEAT **WH**en i lik**E**. i have

poetic **licence**!

don't question me**?**?**?**?

Benjamin Zephaniah

Benjamin Zephaniah was born in Birmingham in 1958. He is a performance poet, actor, writer and radio and TV presenter. He has recently written his first novel, *Face*.

Introduction as a class

Listen carefully while your teacher reads you the poem by E. E. Cummings on **Worksheet 88**. Think about what makes this poem unusual and what you think the poet is trying to say after one reading of the poem.

Development as a group

Your teacher will divide the class into eight groups and give each group one verse of E. E. Cummings' poem to focus on (**Worksheet 89**). Your task is to analyse Cummings' use of language within your verse and what it adds to the meaning of the poem. To help you, watch and listen carefully while your teacher analyses the opening verse for you (see page 115). The question marks indicate tentative suggestions. When you have sorted out your ideas, annotate an OHP version of your verse so you can present your ideas to the class.

Sound effects – rhythm

- Opening lines have sing song, up and down rhythm as indicated by stressed syllables
- Breaks rhythm with list of seasons in steady rhythm – suggests passage of time and repetitive nature of life? Acts as a sort of chorus or refrain – repeated in a slightly different form in later verses

Sound effects

Uses assonance and alliteration to add to repetition within verse?

- Lots of **o** and **ow** sounds give opening a hollow ring
- Repeated **ds** in last line

anyone lived in a pretty **how** town
(with up so floating many bells down)
spring summer autumn winter
he sang his **didn't** he danced his **did**.

General comment:

Can't be certain what each line means but gives overall impression of someone living in a rather boring town and doing the same sort of things year in year out

Syntax

Some lines break rules of English grammar.

- adverb **how** used as if it's an adjective – there to bring out ow sound?
- **didn't** and **did** should be verbs but positioned as if nouns – suggests life full of repetitive actions?

---

as a class

Discuss the following questions:

1 What do you think the poet is trying to say now that you have analysed the poem?
2 Cummings chose to work outside traditional language rules in this poem. Why do you think he has done this?
3 What ingredients has Cummings used in this poem?
4 What makes the poem effective?

> **syntax** the grammatical rules of a language; also, the way in which words and phrases are arranged to form sentences

Plenary

How does the form of a poem contribute to its meaning?

The Speaking and Listening Challenge

Fill in the second section of your speaking and listening record (**Worksheet 87a**).

Inspired by art

Aims

On these two pages you will:

- Compare the ways in which three different poets have been inspired by art.
- Think about the connections between poetry and art.

Starter **as a group**

Look at each of the three paintings on page 117 in turn and brainstorm your responses to the following questions:

1 What do you think each one is about?

2 What do you think each artist's purpose was when they chose to paint their painting in this manner?

3 What have artists and poets got in common?

4 Is there anything about any of these paintings that might inspire someone to write a poem?

Be prepared to feed back your ideas to the class.

Introduction **as a class**

Look at Pieter Brueghel the Elder's painting *Landscape with Fall of Icarus* and see if you can see Icarus.

Now listen carefully while your teacher reads you W. H. Auden's 'Musée des Beaux Arts' (**Worksheet 90**) and see if you can work out what Auden is saying.

Discuss the following questions with a partner before joining the class discussion:

1 What do you think is the purpose of Auden's poem?

2 What ingredients has Auden included to make this poem effective? Use the list from the noticeboard on page 108 to help you.

3 Are there any lines or phrases that you think are particularly effective?

Development **as a group**

Now listen carefully while your teacher reads you two very different poems that were inspired by the other two paintings illustrated on page 117 (**Worksheets 91** and **92**).

Focus first on the poem about Uccello's *Saint George and the Dragon* and then on the poem about Miró's painting.

See if you can answer these questions about each poem in turn:

1 What do you think is the purpose of this poem?

2 How does this differ from Auden's purpose in 'Musée des Beaux Arts'?

3 What ingredients has the poet included to make this poem effective?

4 Are there any lines or phrases that you think are particularly effective?

Be prepared to feed back your ideas to the class.

Plenary

Sum up each poet's approach to writing about the painting that inspired their poem.

The Speaking and Listening Challenge

Fill in the third section of your speaking and listening record (**Worksheet 87a**).

Pieter Brueghel the Elder, Landscape with Fall of Icarus

Paolo Uccello, St George and The Dragon

Joan Miró, The Hunter (Catalan Landscape)

Expressing grief

On these two pages you will:

- Compare the way two different poets have used poetry to express grief.
- Write a poem of your own expressing strong emotions.
- Select one of your own poems and decide how to present it in written and word-processed form.

Starter *as a group*

The two emotions that have probably inspired the most poetry are love and grief.

Brainstorm the following question and see what ideas you can come up with.

> Why do many people use poetry as a way to express strong feelings such as love or grief?

Jot your ideas down on your whiteboards or a piece of paper and be prepared to feed them back to the class.

Introduction *as a class*

Listen carefully while your teacher reads you W. H. Auden's 'Funeral Blues' and think about what makes this such a powerful poem.

Funeral Blues

Stop all the clocks, cut off the telephone,
Prevent the dog from barking with a juicy bone,
Silence the pianos and with muffled drum
Bring out the coffin, let the mourners come.

Let aeroplanes circle moaning overhead
Scribbling on the sky the message He Is Dead
Put crepe bows round the white necks of the public doves,
Let the traffic policemen wear black cotton gloves.

He was my North, my South, my East and West,
My working week and my Sunday rest,
My noon, my midnight, my talk, my song;
I thought that love would last for ever: I was wrong.
The stars are not wanted now; put out every one;
Pack up the moon and dismantle the sun;
Pour away the ocean and sweep up the wood.
For nothing now can ever come to any good.

W. H. Auden

in pairs

Discuss the following questions with a partner before joining the class discussion:

1 What ingredients has Auden included to make this poem effective?

2 Are there any lines or phrases that you think are particularly effective?

Now listen carefully to the extract from Tony Harrison's poem 'Long Distance' on page 119.

as a group

Discuss the following questions in groups and jot down your ideas before joining the class discussion:

1 What ingredients has Harrison included to make this poem effective?

2 Are there any lines or phrases that you think are particularly effective?

3 In what ways does Harrison's poem differ from Auden's?

Though my mother was already two years dead
Dad kept her slippers warming by the gas,
Put hot water bottles her side of the bed
And still went to renew her transport pass.

You couldn't just drop in. You had to phone.
He'd put you off an hour to give him time
To clear away her things and look alone
As though his still raw love were such a crime.

He couldn't risk my blight of disbelief
Though sure that very soon he'd hear her key
Scrape in the rusted lock and end his grief.
He knew she'd just popped out to get the tea.

I believe life ends with death, and that is all.
You haven't both gone shopping; just the same,
In my new black leather phone book there's
   your name
And the disconnected number I still call.

Tony Harrison

Tony Harrison was born in Leeds in 1937. He taught at universities in Nigeria and Czechoslovakia but has for many years made a living as a poet. His poems focus on class, language and power.

Development on your own

Now it's your turn to write about something that you have felt strongly about – it could be pleasant, like winning a game or receiving good news, or sad like the death of someone – or a pet – you love, or something that makes you feel angry. If you like, you could write about someone else's feelings. Or your poem could be about something that has inspired you, such as a painting.

What form will best suit your ideas – the freedom of free verse (William Carlos Williams' approach) or the discipline of more traditional form (such as a sonnet)?

Use your whiteboard or spare paper to jot down your initial ideas.

! **Remember** to read your work carefully, improve it if necessary and write a brief comment on how well you think you have completed the task.

Plenary

Sum up the differences in the way each poet has chosen to write about grief.

The Speaking and Listening Challenge

Fill in the fourth section of your speaking and listening record (**Worksheet 87b**).

homework

Look through all the poems that you have written for this section and select the one you like best. Improve it, if you think it needs improving. Decide how this poem should be presented to maximize its effectiveness. Lay out this poem ready for display in handwritten or word-processed form and decide what presentational devices you will use to give it most impact.

In your book write a brief comment about why you made the decisions that you did in relation to both your choice of poem and its presentation.

Preparing to write an essay

Aims

On these two pages you will:

- Think about how to prepare to write a formal essay.
- Compare the theme and style of two poems by different poets.
- Use an analysis grid to help you record, develop and analyse your ideas.

Starter  as a group

English literature examiners often ask **compare and contrast** questions which go something like this:

> Compare and contrast X's 'Title of poem' with Y's 'Title of poem' and comment on which one you found more effective.

Assuming that you have not read the poems, before you could begin writing such an essay, a series of preparations would be necessary.

Some ideas have been jotted at random on the noticeboard below. Using **Worksheet 93**, sort these ideas out into a sensible order so that you set about your preparations in a logical way.

Introduction as a class

Listen carefully while your teacher reads you Seamus Heaney's poem 'Death of a Naturalist' (page 121), and think about the writer's purpose, theme, narrative perspective, form and style.

Discuss as a class how to fill in the analysis grid for 'Death of a Naturalist' on **Worksheet 94**.

> **compare and contrast** look at the similarities and differences between two texts, ideas, methods or events, etc.

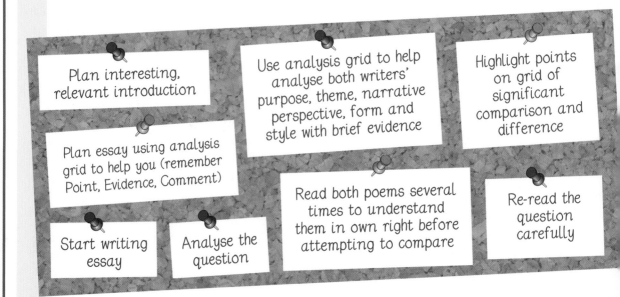

Plan interesting, relevant introduction

Use analysis grid to help analyse both writers' purpose, theme, narrative perspective, form and style with brief evidence

Highlight points on grid of significant comparison and difference

Plan essay using analysis grid to help you (remember Point, Evidence, Comment)

Read both poems several times to understand them in own right before attempting to compare

Re-read the question carefully

Start writing essay

Analyse the question

Death of a Naturalist

All year the flax-dam[1] festered in the heart

Of the townland; green and heavy headed

Flax had rotted there, weighted down by huge sods.

Daily it sweltered in the punishing sun.

Bubbles gargled delicately, bluebottles

Wove a strong gauze of sound around the smell.

There were dragon-flies, spotted butterflies,

But best of all was the warm thick slobber

Of frogspawn that grew like clotted water

In the shade of the banks. Here, every spring

I would fill jampotfuls of the jellied

Specks to range on window-sills at home,

On shelves at school, and wait and watch until

The fattening dots burst into nimble

Swimming tadpoles. Miss Walls would tell us how

The daddy frog was called a bullfrog

And how he croaked and how the mammy frog

Laid hundreds of little eggs and this was

Frogspawn. You could tell the weather by frogs too

For they were yellow in the sun and brown

In rain.

Then one hot day when fields were rank[2]

With cowdung in the grass the angry frogs

Invaded the flax-dam; I ducked through hedges

To a coarse croaking that I had not heard

Before. The air was thick with a bass chorus.

Right down the dam gross-bellied frogs were cocked

On sods; their loose necks pulsed like sails. Some hopped:

The slap and plop were obscene threats. Some sat

Poised like mud grenades, their blunt heads farting.

I sickened, turned and ran. The great slime kings

Were gathered there for vengeance and I knew

That if I dipped my hand the spawn would clutch it.

Seamus Heaney

[1] *reservoir of water where the plant flax grows*
[2] *foul-smelling*

Seamus Heaney was born in 1939 in Castledawson, County Derry, Northern Ireland, the son of a Catholic farmer. Disturbed by the outbreak of violence in the province, he moved to the Republic of Ireland in 1972. His poems focus on the landscape, culture and politics of Ireland. He was awarded the Nobel Prize for literature in 1995.

Development *as a group*

Listen carefully while your teacher reads you Carol Ann Duffy's poem 'In Mrs Tilscher's Class' (**Worksheet 95**), and think about the writer's purpose, theme, narrative perspective, form and style.

Discuss the poem in groups and fill in the analysis grid for 'In Mrs Tilscher's Class' (**Worksheet 96**). Be prepared to feed back your ideas to the class.

Plenary

What are the key points of comparison and contrast between the two poems?

The Speaking and Listening Challenge

Fill in the fifth section of your speaking and listening record (**Worksheet 87b**).

Comparing two poems

Aims

On these two pages you will:

- Plan your formal essay comparing the theme and style of two poems.
- Write a fluent, legible, timed essay in Standard English with the formality suited to reader and purpose.
- Support your points in the essay with effective use of quotation.
- Review your ability to write for a range of purposes and audiences, including your ability to shape ideas rapidly into cohesive paragraphs, and identify targets for further development.

Starter  as a class

This is the essay you are going to write today:

> Compare and contrast Seamus Heaney's 'Death of a Naturalist' with Carol Ann Duffy's 'In Mrs Tilscher's Class' and comment on which one you find more effective.

As you know, formal essays should be written in formal English. This normally means writing in the third person.

- Which aspect of the question above invites you to make personal comment?
- Which part of this essay is, therefore, liable to include comments written in the first person?

If you start off your essay informally, the chances are you will continue writing in the wrong register. Each group will be given the opening of 16 sentences that were written in response to the question above (**Worksheet 97**). Sort them into the two categories below. Be prepared to explain the reasons for your selection.

- Sentence starters that are appropriate for this formal essay
- Sentence starters that are NOT appropriate for this formal essay.

Introduction as a class

Many essays ramble on in an aimless direction. Planning solves this problem.

You have done all the analysis necessary for writing your essay. Now look at the key points of comparison and difference between the two poems that the class drew up at the end of last lesson.

Highlight the aspects of the analysis grid for each poem (**Worksheets 94** and **96**) that will help you make these points and the evidence that will help you support these points. (Remember: Point, Evidence, Comment.) Decide on a logical order for your points – you might find the order of the analysis grid will do, or you may want to alter it to fit the nature of the poems.

The grid can be used in two ways (see box, page 123). Listen carefully while your teacher explains the advantages and disadvantages of each approach.

Select the approach that you feel most confident with and be clear about the key points you want to make. Decide how you are going to introduce your essay.

Approach 1	Approach 2
Introduce both poems, relating introduction to question asked.	Introduce both poems, relating introduction to question asked.
Focus on one poem. Begin with writer's purpose and then go through poem bringing out key thematic and stylistic points as outlined in analysis grid.	Go through both poems, focusing on the key aspects in turn: <ul><li>Writer's purpose and theme</li><li>Narrative approach and tone</li><li>Form, including rhythm and rhyme</li><li>Style – choice of language, image and sound effects</li><li>How poems conclude.</li></ul>
Focus on second poem in similar manner, referring back to first poem and bringing out key points of comparison or difference.	
Personal comment on which poem you found more effective.	Personal comment on which poem you found more effective.
Conclusion summing up key points of comparison and contrast.	Conclusion summing up key points of comparison and contrast.

Development on your own

Your teacher will now set you a time limit within which to write your essay. Read the advice box on timed essays (right) before you start writing.

> **!** **Remember** to read your work carefully. Have you used Standard English throughout? Have you 'flexed your PECs' when making use of quotations from the poems? Improve your essay if necessary and write a brief comment on how well you think you have completed the task.

Plenary

What are the key ingredients of successful formal essay writing?

homework

This section has involved you in a wide range of writing activities. Use **Worksheet 98** to review what progress you have made in these different activities and decide what skills need further development.

All in good time

Use your time wisely. Writing to time is a learnable skill. Not finishing will lose you marks unnecessarily.

Follow these points to make the most of your time:

- Work out before you start when your time limit will be up.
- Check the time roughly every 15 minutes and glance at your plan so you know how much you still have to cover in what time.
- If you are running out of time, sum up the key points you still have to make – the more relevant key points you have made, the better your mark will be.
- Ensure that you have concluded your essay coherently.
- Leave a few minutes to read your work through so that you can correct any careless errors.

Aims

On these two pages you will:
- Discuss how the class can be divided into different groups to present their evaluation of different poems.

Starter *on your own*

In this unit you have read 14 poems. Over the next two lessons you will be involved in organizing the class into working groups and then working in those groups so that different groups can present one of the poems that they liked best. First of all you will need to know which poems everyone preferred. Without discussing your choice with anyone else, fill in **Worksheet 99** to help provide the information the class will need.

When my love swears that she is made of truth,
I do believe her though I know she lies ...

Sonnet 138 by William Shakespeare

Not only marble but the plastic toys
From cornflake packets will outlive this rhyme ...

Sonnet by Wendy Cope

You could travel up the Blue Nile
with your finger, tracing the route ...

'In Mrs Tilscher's Class'
by Carol Ann Duffy

I have *poetic* licence, i wri**T**e th**E** way i wa**Nt**.
i *drop* my **full stops** when *i* like...

'According to my Mood' *by Benjamin Zephaniah*

anyone lived in a pretty how town
(with up so floating many bells down) ...

'anyone lived in a pretty how town'
by E. E. Cummings

About suffering they were never wrong,
The Old Masters: how well they understood ...

'Musée des Beaux Arts' by W. H. Auden

I have eaten
the plums ...

'This Is Just to Say'
by William Carlos Williams

Though my mother was already two years dead
Dad kept her slippers warming by the gas ...

'Long Distance' by Tony Harrison

Not my best side, I'm afraid.
The artist didn't give me a chance to ...

'Not My Best Side' by U. A. Fanthorpe

'I'm rising five,' he said.
'Not four,' and little coils of hair ...

'Rising Five' by Norman Nicholson

Stop all the clocks, cut off the telephone,
Prevent the dog from barking with a juicy bone ...

'Funeral Blues' by W. H. Auden

All year the flax-dam festered in the heart
Of the townland; green and heavy headed ...

'Death of a Naturalist' by Seamus Heaney

so much depends
upon ...

'The Red Wheelbarrow'
by William Carlos Williams

I would like to be a dot in a painting by Miró.
Barely distinguishable from other dots, it's true, but quite uniquely placed ...

'I Would Like to be a Dot in a Painting by Miró' by Moniza Alvi

Introduction _as a group_

The first problem you have to solve in your groups is this:

- The class needs to be divided up into groups of three or four according to their choice of poems.
- As many people as possible should be in a group that is focusing on the poem that was their first choice.
- Everyone should be in a group focusing on one of their top three choices.
- There should be a maximum of two groups working on any one poem.
- As far as possible, people should be working in groups they do not normally work in.

The only information you will have to work on is the poetry preference sheets that you have just filled in (**Worksheet 99**). Using the information on these forms, how would you go about organizing the class into the appropriate groups of three or four? You have five minutes to come up with your group's proposal.

Be prepared to present your ideas coherently and briefly to the class.

as a class

Listen to the various suggestions, decide which is the most likely to succeed, and see if you can organize yourselves efficiently as a class to get yourselves into groups using the chosen method.

Development _as a group_

Working in the groups that you have just established, your task is now the following:

Plan how your group will present your chosen poem to the class, including how you would display it visually, to bring out its best qualities and show how it is effective.

Rules of the exercise

- All group members must take part in the presentation.
- Your presentation should last three to four minutes.
- Do not confer with other groups.
- You may use some of the poems written by people in the class that have been inspired by the poem you are presenting.

Make certain that everyone is clear about their role within the presentation.

Plenary

If you were writing a list of 'dos and don'ts' to help groups work together productively, what would your key 'dos and don'ts' be?

The Speaking and Listening Challenge

Fill in the sixth and seventh sections of your speaking and listening record (**Worksheet 87b**).

Presenting a favourite poem

Aims

On these two pages you will:

- Discuss how to refine your group's presentation.
- Watch all the groups' presentations and evaluate them.
- Reflect on your development as a speaker and listener throughout this section and identify areas for improvement.

Starter

Your group has a few minutes in which to refine your presentation so that it is ready for delivery. Have a rehearsal so that everyone is sure of their role. Use the rules of successful presentation below to help with your performance. If you are reading your chosen poem out loud, read it clearly using the expression appropriate to the poem.

Five rules for successful presentation

- Look at the audience.
- Speak with expression.
- Make your points clearly and fluently.
- Use the appropriate level of formality.
- Do not read from your notes (at most use prompt cards).

Introduction as a class

Each group should present its poem in turn. Make sure that you are a good listener – you will be evaluating your speaking and listening skills at the end of the lesson. Body language is very important, especially when speakers are nervous. Make certain the way you sit and your expression help the presenters to do their best.

As you are watching each presentation, use the evaluation grid on **Worksheet 100** to help you evaluate which presentations are the most effective and why. See what you can learn from others so that you build up your own presentation skills. When you have watched all the presentations, put asterisks against the groups that you think performed best. Be prepared to give reasons for your choice.

Group number & poem focused on	Main strengths of presentation	Key aspects that need improving
Group 1 Auden: 'Musée des Beaux Arts'	1. Clear analysis of the meaning of the poem 2. Everyone was enthusiastic about it in their contribution	1. Slow down a bit! 2. Don't refer to prompt cards so much

Development as a group

Now it's time to evaluate your own contribution to speaking and listening throughout this section. Fill in the final section of your speaking and listening record (**Worksheet 87b**) and follow the instructions in the box below.

Plenary

If you were writing a list of 'dos and don'ts' to help groups make poetry presentations effectively, what would your key 'dos and don'ts' be?

The Speaking and Listening Challenge

- Read through all your entries on your speaking and listening record for this section (**Worksheets 87a–b**) and think about what progress you have made. Look back at **Worksheet 86**, when you evaluated your speaking and listening at the beginning of the section, and set yourself some targets.

- Now fill in **Worksheet 101**, which covers the same ground, to help you evaluate your progress. What differences are there in your self-assessment?

- Finally, set yourself two or three speaking and listening targets based on this evaluation and write them on the back of the worksheet.

Reviewing what's been learnt

In this section you have focused on a wide range of 20th-century poetry. You've looked at poetry ranging from the sonnet with its strict form to free verse with its rejection of rules, and you've experimented with writing your own poetry within these traditions. You've considered some of the fundamental emotions like love and grief and the poetry that they have inspired, and you've thought about how art has inspired poetry. You've decided how best to present visually one of the poems you wrote.

You've compared a variety of poems and particularly focused on how two poets have expressed a child's realization that life is not as innocent as it had seemed. You've strengthened your ability to analyse poetry and plan and write a formal essay, and reviewed your writing skills not just for formal essays but for the wide range of writing skills that this section has included.

You've worked in a group to plan how to organize a series of presentations and worked on your own group presentation of one of the poems that you have enjoyed most. Throughout the section you've developed and recorded your speaking and listening skills, evaluated your progress and set targets for future improvement.

Now it's time to think about what things you have learnt from this section and list the key points in your book, using the following sentence starters to help you:

The things I found most interesting were ...
The things I found most difficult were ...
The things I think I did best were ...
I now feel more confident about ...

You have recently set your writing as well as your speaking and listening targets so now you just have to focus on the remaining key areas:

My targets to improve my work

Reading: This section required some sophisticated analysis of poetry, including comparing ideas, form and style. Look back at your last reading targets and decide what your targets now need to be. You may also want to say which poets you'd like to read more of.

-
-
-

Spelling: Which type of words are still causing you problems? Look at your spelling log and decide what your spelling targets need to be.

-
-
-

Introduction

At the end of Year 9, for the first time since joining your secondary school, you will take the official National Curriculum Tests as specified by the government. These NCTs are an important step in the path of your education and will give you an opportunity to demonstrate the skills and expertise that you have acquired during the last three years. The lessons outlined in the following section will help you to review your skills and prepare you for the tests themselves by taking you through the process and showing you the types of questions that you can expect.

The end of Year 9 is also the time to look forward to the next phase of your education when there will be further challenging opportunities for you to show off your strengths. In Years 10 and 11 you will be working towards taking GCSE examinations in many subjects, including English and English Literature. The last three lessons of this section, therefore, provide an outline of these two GCSE courses; they also include some self-evaluation activities that will help you set goals for the future.

Key aims

In this section you will:

- Learn about the Year 9 National Curriculum Test in English, and practise a range of the questions that are set in both papers of the test.

- Find out about the GCSE English and English Literature courses and set reading and writing targets to help you get on the right track for these courses.

Getting into training

Aims

On these two pages you will:

- Learn about the content and context of the Year 9 National Curriculum Test in English.
- Examine some of the assessment criteria for reading.
- Think about what you can do to prepare for the tests.

Starter  as a class

No athlete just decides to get up one morning and take part in a competition that afternoon. A good deal of training is needed first. Preparing for NC Tests is very similar. You need to make sure that your 'training' – both mental and physical – makes you fit for the challenge. The work that you will be doing in the next few weeks will act as the basis for your training regime.

How to get into training

- Get into the habit of 'feeding your brain' in the morning by eating breakfast.
- Read a selection of articles from quality newspapers and magazines.
- Look up words that you don't know to increase your understanding and vocabulary.
- Examine the way writers use words to create a variety of effects. Just spend a minute or two thinking about this with anything that you read, whatever the context (posters, TV listings … even cereal packets).
- Don't stay up all night swotting – or watching horror films.

in pairs

1 Read together the five helpful hints that have been pinned to the noticeboard below. Discuss how you think each one will help you to do well in the tests.
2 Think of three more helpful hints to share with the class in the feedback session.

Introduction as a class

Around the middle of May in Year 9 you will be taking NC Tests in the three core subjects – English, maths and science. Like the similar groups of tests that you took at the end of Year 6 in primary school, they are national tests, set and marked by external examiners, not by your teachers in school.

These tests are important because they will show how much you have learnt and how much progress you have made during your first three years at secondary school. Preparing for them will help you to review your skills and knowledge. All of this will also be helpful when you start your GCSE courses in September.

Look at **Worksheet 102** as a class; this gives you an outline of what the English papers will contain.

in pairs

Talk about your reactions to what you have just read about the English papers.

- What do you think you will find easy to do?
- What aspects of the test cause you most concern?

Be prepared to feed back to the class.

Development *in pairs*

Your performance in the test will be measured against a range of criteria, which will take account of all your strengths and weaknesses. As a result, you will be given an **NC level**. But what do these levels mean in practice?

Look at the statements that describe students' reading skills on **Worksheet 103**. They have been divided into two sections:

- Statements about students' responses to non-fiction and media texts.
- Statements about students' responses to literature.

In each section the statements describe the reading skills that students should show at each of the NC levels 4 to 8, but they haven't been listed in the right order.

1 Discuss which statements belong to which NC level, and write the level number (4, 5, 6, 7 or 8) in the box.

2 When you have agreed on the right order, highlight the key words in each statement that have helped you to decide the range of difficulty and the progression as you move from one level to another.

Feed back to the class and see if you agree on which statements belong to which level. Your teacher will tell you the correct order.

NC level a National Curriculum level – a grade between 1 and 8 which is given to your work. The average standard expected of students in the Year 9 NCTs is to achieve level 5 or 6. Some will do better than this, attaining levels 6 or 7 (or even level 8 if the extension paper is taken), but for others accomplishing level 3 or 4 is a measure of achievement.

TOP TIPS FOR TACKLING NCTS

- **Read the questions carefully:** make sure you answer the questions that are there, not the ones you'd like to be there.
- Use the information given to you about the time allowed and the number of marks awarded to help you **focus on what is important**. Spend more time on the questions that are awarded more marks, not on the questions that you like.
- **Follow the guidance on the paper** – such as advice listed as bullet points – as it is there to help you.
- Make sure that you **think about your response and plan** what you are going to say before you write.
- **Leave time to read through and correct** what you have written. Don't be afraid to make changes on the paper such as crossing out incorrect spellings, adding more interesting words, etc. Credit is given for your editing skills – it shows that you care.
- **Concentrate on quality, not quantity**. A concise but clear, well-focused response is worth far more than a rambling, confused one.

Remember: If you have been working hard and following your English course attentively for the last three years, you will have nothing to fear. The test is not designed to trick you or catch you out, but to give you an opportunity to show what you can do.

Plenary

What do you need to start doing now to prepare you for the NC Test in English? Write down two things on your whiteboard or a piece of paper.

The shorter reading question

Aims

On these two pages you will:

- Consider how best to use the preparation time at the start of Paper 1.
- Analyse the features of a shorter NCT reading question, and write a response to the question.
- Review what you know about descriptive writing.

Starter

How do writers describe to others what they have seen and felt? In groups of four:

1. Make a list of the language features that you might expect to find in descriptive writing. (For example, powerful adjectives: you should be able to think of at least three more features.)

2. On your own, write an example to show you clearly understand each language feature that you have identified.

3. Share your examples with other members of your group, and be prepared to feed back to the class.

Introduction · as a class

Sections A and B of Paper 1 of the NC English Test give you an opportunity to demonstrate your skills in understanding and analysing two texts. The questions usually focus on the devices used by the author to capture the attention of the reader. This could include such things as examining the title and opening paragraph, discussing the use of adjectives and imagery, and analysing the writer's style and narrative technique. *Remember that it is your reading skills that are being assessed, not your writing expertise.*

In the test you will have 15 minutes' reading time before you can start writing your responses. Make sure that while you are reading the passages, you also begin to analyse them, and that you analyse the questions carefully, in preparation for writing your response later on. (See panel, 'Use your reading time effectively'.)

The passage you are going to study this lesson is an example of the kind of shorter question that may be set in section A or B of Paper 1. You are going to think about the passage and the questions on it carefully so that you are fully prepared when you write the answer for homework.

As a class, read the extract on **Worksheet 104** about Fanny Kemble's trip on Stephenson's *Rocket*, the first railway locomotive, in 1830. In order to analyse a piece of writing, you need to have a clear idea about what type of writing you are examining. As you read through the extract, therefore, ask yourselves these questions:

- What is the purpose, form and audience of the extract? Why was it written? What type of writing do you think it is? What was the intended audience?

- What features of the writing help you to come to your conclusions? Find some examples in the text to support your views.

Be prepared to feed back your ideas to the class.

Use your reading time effectively

How can you make best use of the 15 minutes' reading time that you are given at the start of each paper? Follow these four steps:

1 Read the extract through once and try to build up an idea of its purpose, form and audience.

2 Read the questions under the extract and analyse what they are asking you to do. Highlight the key words in the question so that the focus of your answer stands out clearly.

3 Read the extract through again, this time looking for the specific features identified in the question. Use highlighters to help you pick out points that you can use when you write your answer.

4 Examine the bullet points under the question. They are there to guide you and help you plan your answer. You may even like to address each bullet point in turn, making each one a new paragraph.

Development **in pairs**

Read the question beneath the extract. It asks you to focus on the *descriptive language* skills used by the writer to tell others about her experience. It does *not* ask you simply to retell the story of what happened. To help you avoid falling into this trap, follow steps 2 to 4 outlined in the panel 'Use your reading time effectively'. Talk with your partner about what you have found.

● What are the key words in the question? Write them down and don't forget what they are.

● Look for the key points in the extract that will help you answer the question.

● Use highlighters to pick out the descriptive words, phrases and imagery used by the author.

● Examine the bullet points and discuss which ones relate to the examples you have highlighted in the passage.

Be prepared to feed back to the class.

on your own

1 Look at the evidence that you have now selected.

2 Decide which examples you will use to address each of the points you have been asked to focus on, both in the question and in the bullet points. Choose only the best examples, as you won't have time to mention everything in 20 minutes.

3 Plan your answer. Make sure that you cover the bullet points, either by addressing each bullet point in turn or by using a different plan of your own that covers the points.

Having planned your answer, you are now ready to write.

Plenary

What should you be doing in your 15 minutes' reading time at the start of the NC Test? What should you *not* be doing?

homework

In no more than 20 minutes answer the question on the passage on **Worksheet 104**.

> **!** **Remember** to read your work carefully – have you covered all the bullet points? Improve it if necessary.

The longer reading question

Aims

On these two pages you will:

- Study a longer NCT reading question, and write a response to the question in timed conditions.
- Review strategies for increasing your understanding of unfamiliar words.

Starter as a group

Often the test passages will contain words that you do not recognize, or words whose meaning is not quite clear. In a test situation you would not be able to ask anyone for help or use a dictionary.

The words given below come from the test passage that you will be studying this lesson:

static	adjacent
contour	prevailing
whorls	sibling
embankment	orienteer
gradient	lichen-crusted

1. In groups, make a list of the ways in which you can try to work out the meaning of any of these words, such as studying prefixes, word roots and word families.
2. These words have been highlighted on the passage itself (**Worksheet 105a**). How can using the context help you to understand their meaning?
3. Some of you will know the meanings of these words already. Between you pool your knowledge and explain each of the words.

Be prepared to feed back to the class.

Introduction

This lesson you are going to be looking at an example of a longer passage of the type you might expect to find in Paper 1 in your NC Test. As it is a longer passage, two questions are set on it. Like many of the passages, this one comes from a broadsheet newspaper. This information should enable you to identify the purpose, form and audience with relative ease. You should also expect the general vocabulary level of the writing to be quite high as it has not been adapted for a younger audience.

Remember the strategies that you practised last lesson: these will help you to plan your answer in an efficient and organized way.

in pairs

Make a list of what you should do *before* you start to write your responses.

Feed back to the class.

on your own

You have **10 minutes** to:

- Read the passage on **Worksheets 105a–b**
- Read the questions given on page 135
- Start planning your response (remember what you learnt last lesson).

Remember that you must not start writing your response until you are told to.

Read the passage on **Worksheets 105a–b.**

*Then answer question 1 and question 2. (Remember to spend about **10 minutes** on question 1 and **20 minutes** on question 2.)*

This passage is a report from a newspaper, The Guardian. It is about a biking holiday that the journalist had with his family in the Peak District.

1 Look again at the **first two paragraphs** of the passage (lines 3 to 17).

How does the writer engage the interest of his reader in the first two paragraphs of the passage?

In your answer you should comment on:

- the effect created through the use of the first and second person

- the way in which the writer uses direct speech, tone and subject matter to capture the reader's attention.

*Refer to words and phrases in the **first two paragraphs** to support your ideas.*

6 marks

2 Look again at the remaining part of the passage from **paragraph three to the end** (lines 18 to 81).

How does the writer persuade the reader that cycling in the Peak District is an enjoyable and worthwhile holiday for a family?

In your answer you should comment on:

- the writer's choice of words and phrases that makes the cycling trip sound like effortless fun

- the way in which the writer describes the scenery

- the writer's attention to the educational aspects of the journey

- the information that the writer has selected for his readers.

*Refer to words and phrases from **paragraph three to the end of the passage** to support your ideas.*

11 marks

Development on your own

You now have 30 minutes to answer questions 1 and 2.

! **Remember** the guidance you have been given about how to divide your time between the two questions. Read your work carefully – have you covered all the bullet points? Improve it if necessary.

Plenary

Share with the class what you have learnt from the experience of doing this exercise under proper timed conditions.

Set yourself two targets to aim for when working under strict timed conditions in the future.

Aims

On these two pages you will:

- Study an NCT writing question and discuss how you would plan your response.
- Write a response to the question, making effective use of descriptive detail.
- Explore the performance criteria for writing and use them to assess students' writing.
- Identify areas of spelling that you need to improve and use strategies to help you eliminate persistent errors.

Starter  on your own

Everyone has their own nightmare spellings which still seem to trip them up: which letters are doubled in 'occasionally'? How many 'c's and 's's are there in 'necessary'? Is there an 'e' or an 'a' in independent? You know the sort of thing.

Under test conditions you have only the words on the question paper and those stored in your brain to help – no dictionaries or spelling logs will be there to help you. If you want to achieve level 5 and above it is important that you spell both complex and common words accurately.

 Look through some of your recent written work in English or other subjects; better still, look at your spelling log.

1   Pick out ten words that are your most common errors.

2   Check how to spell each one correctly, using a dictionary.

3   For each one, examine what it is

that you are getting wrong.

4   Put the words into different groups, such as double letters, i before e, missing syllables, etc.

5   Make a point of learning the correct spelling (perhaps a partner could help you), using the repertoire of spelling strategies that you should by now have built up.

Be ready to be tested on these words in the next lesson.

> Note: spelling common words is important, but you will also be given credit for using interesting words from a wider vocabulary, even if they are not spelt correctly, so don't be afraid to use expressive and colourful words in your writing.

Introduction

Section C of Paper 1 in your NC Test gives you an opportunity to demonstrate your writing skills. You will be given three options to choose from. Remember to **answer only one**. (If you do any more than this the examiner just marks the first one and puts a line through the extra work.) The fact that you are given choices means that you need to think about what you would be able to do best. But don't spend too long choosing as you don't have much time.

The writing questions will look something like the one given on page 137.

 in pairs

Discuss the questions below with your partner:

1   How does the information provided in the question help and guide you as a writer?

a) Writers and journalists like Fanny Kemble and Dan Joyce, whose work you read in sections A and B, have shared their experiences in a way that successfully engages the interest of their readers.

Write about a memorable journey that you have made.

In your writing you could:

- inform your reader by selecting details concerning the journey, such as where you went and the method of transport used, which you think will interest them

- describe what you saw and how you felt about the journey

- explain why this experience has remained with you and why you remember it so clearly.

Try to give the reader a real sense of what your experience was like through your choice of detail and use of language.

33 marks

2 If you were to write a response to this task what would be the purpose, form and audience for your writing? How would this influence your chosen style and tone?

3 What are the key clues given to you in the bullet points that should be used to guide your writing?

4 How would you make your writing interesting to your audience? Give some actual examples of techniques and devices that you could use.

5 In the real test you will have only 35 minutes to plan and write your response. How would this influence your approach?

Be prepared to feed back your ideas to the class.

Development *as a group*

Now place yourself in the role of someone marking, or assessing, what you have written. What do you think would be the main criteria that they would use to consider the achievement of the writer?

In groups, read through the performance criteria that are used to assess students' answers to this question (**Worksheet 106**). Then read the opening paragraphs of four students' answers on **Worksheet 107**.

1 Comment on each one and say how it relates to the performance criteria.

2 Put the four extracts in order of merit from the worst to the best.

3 Discuss the level that you think would be appropriate for each one.

Be prepared to feed back to the class. Do you all agree?

Plenary

Using your whiteboard or a piece of paper, write down three things that you must remember about the writing question in the NC Test.

homework

Write your response to the writing question above. Take no more than 35 minutes to complete it.

! **Remember** to read your work carefully – have you made good use of descriptive detail to make your writing interesting? Improve it if necessary.

The writing question (2)

Aims

On these two pages you will:

- Act as a critical friend, reviewing what your partner has written for last lesson's homework.
- Attempt a response to an NCT writing question under test conditions, using the appropriate degree of formality and writing fluently and accurately.
- Test your spelling of words that cause you persistent problems.

Starter  in pairs

1 Test your partner's spelling of the ten 'nightmare' words that they identified last lesson.

2 Reverse roles.

3 Check how well you have both done.

4 If there are still some mistakes, think of strategies that will help your partner to remember the words that are still causing problems.

Feed back to the class – who got ten out of ten?

Introduction in pairs

This lesson you will attempt a writing task under exam conditions. First, though, you are going to review what your partner has written for the previous lesson's homework. This should give you a chance to receive a bit of last-minute advice from a critical friend.

You have no more than **7 minutes** to complete these tasks:

1 Read the writing that your partner completed for the previous lesson's homework.

2 Highlight, or put a tick by, three things that you like about what they have written – it could be an unusual descriptive phrase, an element of humour or something in the subject matter itself that catches your attention.

3 Circle one thing that could be improved – changing a simple sentence into a complex one, suggesting a more imaginative word for a dull one, or indicating where an idea could be developed.

4 Talk to each other about the points you have drawn out above.

Development on your own

In the next 35 minutes you will be completing a writing task under test conditions to see what you can actually do in the time that is allocated to you in the NC Test.

Before you attempt the task (on **Worksheet 108**), remind yourself of the points on the notice board on page 139.

Plenary

Share with the class what you have learnt from the experience of writing to time.

- What writing option did you choose and why?
- What strategies did you apply to engage the interest of the audience?
- Did you finish?

TOP TIPS FOR TACKLING THE WRITING QUESTION

- Spend about five minutes planning before you start to write.
- Identify clearly the audience, purpose and form of what you are about to write.
- Begin in a way that immediately indicates you are aware of the purpose and form of your writing.
- Make a deliberate effort to engage the attention and interest of your reader.
- Ensure that your style and tone are appropriate.

- Use as wide and varied a vocabulary as you can, and a variety of sentence structures to create different effects.
- Organize and develop your paragraphs in a logical way.
- Check that you have spelt common words correctly.
- Make sure that your handwriting is clear.
- It is important to finish the question, even if you have to do this in note form because you run out of time.

Aims

On these two pages you will:

- Review what you know about the set scenes from *Macbeth*.
- Explore the type of question that is given in Paper 2 of your NC Test.
- Consider what factors to take into account when choosing a question to answer.
- Plan your answer to the question you have chosen.

Starter  on your own

Before you take your NC Test on Shakespeare (Paper 2) you must know the text, especially your given scenes, very well. Your teacher will give you a quiz to test your knowledge of *Macbeth* (**Worksheet 109**). Listen to the instructions before you do the quiz.

- How well did you do?
- How much revision do you still need to do?

Introduction

Paper 2 of the NCT in English tests your response to literature, namely Shakespeare. This test is **one hour and 15 minutes long**, and in that time you have to complete **one task** on the play you have studied (there are two questions from the set scenes on each play for you to choose from).

You will be given a copy of the scenes you have studied in a booklet with the relevant scenes from the other two plays that have also been set for study. Make sure that you locate the

ones that relate to you early. However, you need to remember that these will be plain texts with no notes or annotations. (You may not take any of your own texts into the test.)

In addition you will be given a question paper and a booklet in which to write your answers. The question paper contains questions on all three plays, so again it is important to make sure that you go straight to those that relate to the play that you have studied.

 in pairs

Study the two questions that have been set on *Macbeth* and examine the way they are set out (**Worksheet 110**). Then discuss these questions in pairs:

1 What guidance are you given to help you write your response?

2 How should you use the clues that are there?

on your own

You are given a choice of two questions. Making the right choice is very important. Spend time looking closely at both options: don't just go for the one that seems more attractive – often in the end it isn't. For example, a question that asks you to write in role as a producer may appear attractive, but there is a danger that you might forget to make close reference to the text or to use quotations.

Look at the questions you have been given again, this time while considering the following issues:

- What type of response is needed? For example, comparative, discursive, argumentative, imaginative, factual?

- Are you being asked to write in role, in the first person, perhaps as a producer or a character?

- What do you need to know before you can answer the question? Do you have this knowledge? For example, plot or language analysis, examination of a theme or a character.

- Which scene or aspect of the play are you being asked to focus on?

- Have you been asked to give a judgement, offer an opinion or give a personal point of view?

When you have thought about these issues, choose which question you would answer. Be prepared to give the reasons for your choice to the class.

Development on your own

In this test there is time to plan, think and find your evidence, but it is important that you use your time wisely. The examiners will not expect you to rush through your work. You need to show that you have put thought into your response.

Focus on the question you have chosen and begin to plan your response. Listen carefully while your teacher reads you the advice in the panel opposite.

Plenary

Without looking at the textbook, write on your whiteboard or a piece of paper one important point that you have learnt about how to *choose* your response to a Shakespeare question, and one important point about how to *plan* your response.

PLANNING YOUR ANSWER

Analyse the question thoroughly – look for key words and hints about what you need to consider and include in your response. Highlight them so that they stand out clearly.

Study the text of the scene on which the question has been based. By now the text should be so familiar that you will be scanning it for evidence that you know, highlighting points that are relevant.

Find and select appropriate quotations – evidence drawn from the text is very important, but remember to keep the examples brief and to the point. Choose only the best examples.

Point, evidence, comment (PEC) – remember that quotations have to be used effectively, they are not an end in themselves. Their value lies in the points that you are making and the comments that you make to support these points.

Structure your response according to the main question that has been asked. If you like, use the bullet points as a guide to remind you of the areas you should cover, but the organization should depend on your personal style and preference.

Include personal points of view. Never be afraid to say 'I think'. It is important to show that you have a considered point of view that you can support, rather than simply repeating things that you have been told to say.

The Shakespeare paper (2)

Aims

On these two pages you will:

- Attempt a question from Paper 2 of the NC Test by writing an essay in Standard English in a given time period.
- Review some terms that are useful for analysing drama.

Starter  in pairs

Can you remember what these terms mean?

quotation	dramatic irony
character	act
verse	scene
prose	dialogue
soliloquy	tragedy

Discuss the words and their meaning with a partner. Be prepared to feed back to the class.

Introduction on your own

In the previous lesson you were given an NC Test question to examine and prepare. This will have helped you to understand the approach that you need to adopt and the implications of the time allocation. During this lesson you will be given a test question to answer on your own. First of all read the advice box on page 143 carefully.

Your teacher will give you two questions on *Macbeth* (**Worksheet 111**), as well as the relevant parts of the scenes for you to use as support material.

In the next 15 minutes:

- Study the questions carefully and choose one of them.
- Select your evidence.
- Plan the points you wish to make.

Development on your own

Begin to write your answer in its final form.

Your teacher will give you directions about time allocation and completion, so listen carefully.

> **!** **Remember** to read your work carefully – have you covered all the bullet points? Improve it if necessary.

Plenary

On your whiteboard or a piece of paper, write down three things that you think you need to do to improve your performance in the real NC Test. Be prepared to share these in a class discussion.

homework

Your teacher may ask you to complete the essay that you have started in class.

Top tips for writing about Shakespeare in your NC Test

Before the test:

- Make sure that you **know your set scenes very well**.
- Examine and understand the **role of each character** in the set scenes.
- Ensure that you know the sequence of events in the set scenes.

During the planning stage in the test:

- **Think carefully before making your choice** between the two questions.
- **Pick out the key words in your chosen question** and maintain your focus on them throughout the test.
- Use the **bullet points** given after the questions as guidance to support your answer and make sure that you cover all the issues that they suggest.
- Consider the **visual aspects of the play** – never forget that it is a performance (don't refer to the play as a book or a video).

When writing your response:

- Always **state clearly which question you are answering** by writing the number and/or title at the top of the page.
- Remember to flex your PECs: **point, evidence, comment**.
- When you are writing about the play, underline its title or put it in inverted commas (<u>Macbeth</u> or 'Macbeth'), but don't use either method when referring to the characters.
- Adopt a **formal tone** when writing your essay, which should be in Standard English.
- Remember to **paragraph your work, write legibly and spell correctly**.

At the end of the test:

- Always leave time to read through and **check what you have written**.
- If you run out of time, **complete your answer** in note form.

Aims

On these two pages you will:
- Find out about the GCSE English exam.
- Explore the speaking and listening and coursework components of GCSE English.

Starter  as a group

In groups of four, brainstorm your answers to the following questions:

1 What have you most enjoyed about the English lessons and activities during Years 7 to 9?

2 What do you think are some of the most important skills you have learnt?

3 What have you found difficult and would like a chance to improve?

Be prepared to feed back your responses to the class.

Introduction

As you come to the end of Year 9 it is time to think about your two-year **GCSE** course, which leads to examinations in May and June of Year 11. GCSEs are probably the most important set of examinations that you will ever take. Your success in them will help to determine the choices that you can make concerning your further education and the jobs that you can apply for. A good grade in English, such as C, B, A or A* will help to open doors to your future. Whatever you wish to study at university, you must have a good grade in English before you can be accepted.

Read **Worksheet 112** together, which gives an outline of what you can expect of a GCSE course in English. Then discuss these questions:

1 What similarities do you notice between the outline given for GCSE and the Year 9 assessments?

2 What is different to the Year 9 assessments?

Be prepared to feed back to the class.

GCSE General Certificate of Secondary Education. The courses that you will study, leading up to the GCSE examinations in Year 11, will follow the National Curriculum, but will be directed by the particular external exam board that your school has chosen. These are associated with various universities across the country, such as London, Oxford and Cambridge.

Development

Your speaking and listening assessment is an important part of the work that you do through the two years of the GCSE course. Although your teacher assessment at the end of Year 9 would have included an element of speaking and listening, your test result would not. As you undertake your GCSE course in English, remember that your speaking and listening assessment counts for as much as your written coursework, in terms of the proportion of marks contributing to your final grade.

Written coursework is also a vital and integral part of GCSE English. During the next two years some of the work

that you complete on your own – in your own time, rather than under examination conditions – will contribute to your final grade. The type of work that is required is set by the examination board and will include a mixture of personal writing, non-fiction writing and writing about literature, such as Shakespeare, poetry or novels. Your teacher will make it clear to you which pieces of work are being completed as part of your coursework requirement.

Coursework gives you an opportunity to show what you can do when given the time that you need, unlike the rush and constraints of an examination. You need to give it a high priority.

In groups of four, brainstorm the following questions:

1 Why is speaking and listening included as part of the GCSE assessment?

2 What are the advantages of coursework?

3 What are the disadvantages of coursework?

4 Why do you think the examination boards include coursework as part of the final assessment at GCSE?

Be prepared to feed back to the class.

Plenary

Using your whiteboard or a piece of paper, write down the three sources of marks that form your final assessment in GCSE English.

Aims

On these two pages you will:

- Find out about the GCSE English Literature exam.
- Review your own reading preferences.
- Reflect on the reading challenges and goals you can set yourself for the future.

Starter

This lesson you are going to explore the second GCSE English course – English Literature. Of course, there are many types of writing in English – for example, newspaper reports, letters, instructions – so what counts as literature? Literature is a term used to describe writing in the form of drama, prose and poetry, by distinguished authors, whose power arises from the beauty of the language, the expression of ideas and the emotional effect that it may create in the reader.

as a group

Talk about the literature you have read and studied in Years 7 to 9. Select three examples of each of the following types of literature, and say why you liked or disliked them:

- Drama
- Prose
- Poetry.

Be ready to feed back to the class.

Introduction

Apart from GCSE English, most students in Year 11 also take another examination called GCSE English Literature. Although this course is usually studied alongside the straight English course, you achieve two separate GCSEs, with perhaps different grades, at the end of the two years. The grades that are awarded for these two subjects are not linked in any way (as they are for double science, for example, where the same grade is given).

Your own reading experience so far will have broadened your mind, improved your writing skills and opened doors into your imagination, as well as doors for personal development and enjoyment. It will also have helped to give you many of the skills that you will need for the GCSE English Literature course, such as appreciation of the writer's craft, analysis of language and content, comparisons between texts written at the same or different times, character studies, etc.

on your own

In order to help you prepare for the literature GCSE course that you will start next term, it is useful to spend some time reflecting on your own reading. Begin this process by completing the reading self-evaluation on **Worksheet 113**. It may help you to think back to the work you did in the starter activity, when you talked about the different types of literature that you have read and studied so far, as well as your likes and dislikes.

Development as a group

The literature that you will study for GCSE is specified by the National Curriculum and the texts are set by the examination board. It will include poetry, drama and prose (usually novels) by a range of writers, some of them pre-20th century. Some texts will be studied as part of your coursework and some will be examination texts.

As with your Shakespeare play at the end of Year 9, the set texts are examined at the end of the GCSE course. Most examination boards have an 'open book' policy, which means that you can take the texts into the examination, as long as they are not covered in notes. The examination is one of the longest GCSEs; it can be two and a half hours long.

You need to make sure that you understand the difference between exam texts and coursework texts, but the good news is that some of the coursework that you complete for the English Literature course can be doubled up and used as English coursework as well.

on your own

In order to prepare for GCSE English Literature (as well as GCSE English), one of the most useful things you can do is to widen the variety of things that you read and increase their level of difficulty. So set yourself a reading challenge for the summer holidays by completing **Worksheet 114**. (You may need to think about the responses that you gave to the self-evaluation on **Worksheet 113**.)

Plenary

Share your responses to **Worksheets 113** and **114** with a partner.

- Talk about how realistic you have been. Have you been too hard or too easy on yourself?
- As a result of your discussions, make any changes that you think would provide a fairer challenge.

homework

For your holiday homework, prepare to meet the reading challenges and goals you have set yourself on **Worksheet 114**.

Self-evaluation

Aims

On these two pages you will:

- Review your skills in reading and writing.
- Set targets in reading and writing to help you achieve success in your GCSE English course next year.
- Discuss what makes a useful target.

Starter

Now that you have some idea of what the GCSE English and English Literature courses consist of, it only remains to prepare yourself for a promising start by gaining a good understanding of your strengths and recognizing the skills that you need to improve. In the 'Plan, draft, present' section (pages 107–128) you will have assessed your speaking and listening skills and set targets. In this lesson you will be reflecting on your reading and writing skills to help you set future goals.

Throughout Years 7 to 9 you will have set many targets and achieved many of your goals. As you should know, a useful target is a **SMART** target:

- **S**pecific – clearly defined and understood.
- **M**easurable – so that you know if and when the target has been hit.
- **A**chievable – not too difficult, which is discouraging; not too easy, which is a waste of time.
- **R**elevant – to the specific task and audience.
- **T**ime limited – there must be a deadline.

This means you need to include in the target how you are going to achieve the goal. For example: 'This term I will improve the range of my reading *by reading two articles from a quality newspaper once a week.*'

as a group

Read the targets that a Year 9 student set himself (**Worksheet 115**). Bearing in mind the five characteristics of a SMART target, work in groups to grade the targets using the system outlined on the worksheet.

Be prepared to feed back to the class.

Introduction *on your own*

Developing reading skills will help you, not just in English but in all your other subjects as well. So now you are going to reflect on how effective you are as a reader. This is not directly related to your reading of literature, but more to do with skills of understanding and appreciating the things that you read.

1   Use the statements on **Worksheet 116** to guide your assessment of yourself as a reader and give yourself a score of 1 to 5 for each of the statements.

2   Look at the areas where you think your score is lower than it should be, and think about how you could improve your skills in these areas.

3   Set yourself two targets for improving your reading and add them to the bottom of the worksheet. Make sure they are SMART targets.

Be prepared to feed back to the class.

Development on your own

Now it is time to examine your writing skills. As writing is the main method of communicating your knowledge, ideas and understanding in most GCSE subjects, it is a very important skill to master in all its many different forms.

1 Use the statements on **Worksheet 117** to guide your assessment of yourself as a writer and give yourself a score of 1 to 5 for each of the statements.

2 Look at the areas where you think your score is lower than it should be, and think about how you could improve your skills in these areas.

3 Set yourself two targets for improving your writing and add them to the bottom of the worksheet. Make sure they are SMART targets.

Be prepared to feed back to the class.

A word of advice about setting your targets …

When you come to set your targets, don't feel that you have to choose only those things which have low scores. If everything you set yourself to do seems a hard mountain to climb, you may not even feel like taking the first steps towards them.

Consider these approaches:

- In order to feel encouraged, choose something that is small but still significant.

- Think about what is most important to you in terms of the skills you need to have. Concentrate on getting those things right that will be most valuable to you in the future.

- Take the initiative yourself and push yourself towards your goals. They are for YOU, not your teacher, so remember what they are.

	Writing skills	Score
A	I write in a way that takes account of my reader so that I vary my style and vocabulary to suit their needs	
B	I can write in different forms, such as letters, leaflets and essays, for a range of different purposes	
C	I can develop my ideas in organized paragraphs	
D	I can vary the length and construction of my sentences according to the tone and purpose of my writing	

Plenary

Examine the targets that you have set yourself and think of two things that you could do in the holidays that will help to keep your skills alive and ticking. Write them down on your whiteboard or a piece of paper and share them with the class.

homework

In the holidays don't forget to carry out the work that you have set yourself. Be ready to report on your success at the beginning of next term.

Reviewing what's been learnt

Your *English Frameworking* course has come to an end. By now you should be really skilled at reading, writing, speaking and listening: able to read and understand almost anything that takes your interest; able to write with imagination and accuracy in all sorts of different styles and for different purposes; and able to feel confident in any situation that requires you to take on a role or speak and listen to others.

In this section you will have:

- Understood the nature of the Year 9 NC Test in English.
- Prepared yourself to take this test by reviewing your skills and completing practice responses to questions.
- Reviewed the Shakespeare play that you have studied in preparation for Paper 2 of the NC Test.
- Learnt something about the GCSE courses in English and English Literature that you will be taking in the next two years.
- Undertaken some self-assessment activities to help you set future targets.

Remember to keep the targets that you have set yourself so that you can refer to them at the beginning of Year 10.

Glossary

abbreviation a shortened version of a word or group of words. Common abbreviations include 'Mr' (for 'Mister'), Co. (for 'Company') and USA (for 'United States of America'). You can also use your own abbreviations to save space or time when writing notes or diaries.

abstract based on thoughts and ideas rather than physical objects; compare **concrete**

accent the way in which words are pronounced. Accent is determined by where people live, where they were born, their education and social class. Compare **dialect**.

acknowledgement a formal note of the source of a piece of information or of a quotation in a text. Acknowledgements include, as a minimum, the title and author of the text used.

active the 'voice' used when the subject of a sentence performs the action of the verb: 'The police arrested the man.' Compare **passive**.

adjective a word that describes something: 'the tall cupboard', 'the round balloon'

adverb a word or phrase that tells you more about a verb, an adjective or even a whole sentence: 'Leon spoke quietly', 'The brightly coloured shawl', 'I will give it to you tomorrow'

adverbial phrase a group of words that functions in the same way as an adverb: 'by car', 'a few days ago', 'of course', 'in a strange way'

advertisement a text advertising goods or services, especially in newspapers, magazines, television and radio

advice text that advises; words – either spoken or written – that give information or suggestions for how someone should act or behave

advise to offer information and suggestions for how someone should act or behave in a particular situation

agreement having the same opinion about a subject

alliteration the effect created when words next to or close to each other begin with the same letter or sound: 'several silent slithering snakes'

amendment alteration, change, improvement

analyse to look at something in detail as a way of understanding it better

analysis grid a grid which helps you to analyse a text by focusing on the different parts of it

anecdote a short, entertaining story about a person or event

annotate mark up with your own notes, which are usually made in the margin

antonym a word opposite in meaning to another word: 'good' and 'bad' are antonyms. Compare **synonym**.

apostrophe a punctuation mark used to indicate either possession (Tim's book) or omitted letters (can't)

argue to put forward a viewpoint

aside words spoken in an undertone on stage which other actors are not supposed to hear

assessment a formal **evaluation**

assessment focus an aspect of reading or writing that is assessed by an examiner

assonance the effect created by the repetition of vowel sounds: 'green fields'

assumption a belief that something is true, without thinking about it

attainment target a list of the knowledge, skills and understanding that you need to achieve in each subject skill at every level. In English there are three attainment targets, one for each of the special skills: 1 speaking and listening, 2 reading and 3 writing.

audience the group of people watching or listening to a performance, especially of a play or concert; also, people who read or listen to any texts, whether newspapers, television programmes, books or films

aural to do with listening skills; compare **oral**

autobiography an account of a person's life told by themselves; compare **biography**

auxiliary verb a verb such as 'be', 'have' and 'do' which helps in the formation of tenses or questions

balanced not taking sides; a balanced analysis presents information factually without trying to bias the reader towards any viewpoint

ballad see **narrative poem**

biased unfairly presented to favour one point of view over another; see also **subjective**

bibliography the section of a text that lists further reading or acknowledges the sources used

biography an account of a person's life told by someone else; compare **autobiography**

blank verse verse that doesn't rhyme. It often has a regular pattern of ten syllables with five stresses in each line: 'For he to-day that sheds his blood with me'.

broadsheet a larger format newspaper; compare **tabloid**

brochure a booklet that gives information about a product or service

cartoon a drawing or series of drawings which are funny or make a point

CD-ROM a disk used with a computer system which can contain written information, moving and still images and sound

chairperson the person in charge of a debate, who decides when each person may speak

character a person in a novel, short story or play

characterization how characters are described or portrayed by the writer

chronological arranged in the order in which things happened

classification a broad descriptive statement about something. Information texts often begin with a classification: 'Primates are the higher mammals'.

classified advert a small **advertisement**, usually placed in a newspaper by individuals; they are usually arranged in categories (such as 'Situations Vacant') and set out in columns

clause the building block of a sentence; each clause must include a verb and normally includes a subject as well. Some sentences consist of a single clause: 'It was snowing.' Other sentences consist of two or more clauses: 'It was snowing and we were cold.' See also **subordinate clause**.

cliché a phrase or idea that has been used so much that it is no longer effective: 'explore every avenue', 'money doesn't grow on trees'

cliffhanger a situation that keeps the audience guessing what will happen in the next episode of a drama or story

clipped form a word formed from the reduction of another word: 'phone' from 'telephone'

closed question a question that requires a 'yes' or 'no' answer, or an answer limited to a list of choices; compare **open question**

coherence the underlying logic and consistency of a text. In a coherent text the ideas expressed should be relevant to one another so that the reader can follow the meaning.

coherent text is coherent if the ideas expressed are relevant to each other and are presented in a logical way so that the reader can follow the meaning

cohesion the way in which the parts of a text fit together. This is often signposted by grammatical features such as **connectives**.

cohesive a cohesive text is one whose parts fit well together

colloquial to do with conversation. Colloquial language is used in familiar, informal contexts.

comedy of manners a comedy which explores the way in which a particular social group behaves

comment to express a view on something based on an analysis of it

commentary an explanatory series of notes or comments

commercial a television or radio **advertisement**

compare and contrast look at the similarities and differences between two texts, ideas, methods or events, etc.

comparison using different forms of adjectives and adverbs to compare things. When you compare two things or people you add the suffix 'er' or the word 'more': 'Mike was faster, but Lisa was more graceful.' When you compare more than two things or people you add the suffix 'est' or the word 'most': 'It's the nicest house, but also the most expensive.'

complex sentence a sentence containing one main clause and one or more subordinate clauses

complication a problem which adds interest to the plot of a story

compound sentence a sentence made up of two or more main clauses joined by a conjunction such as 'and' or 'but': 'Richard went to the cinema but Ruth went bowling'

conceit an elaborate image or startling comparison

concise dictionary a dictionary which omits the more obscure terms listed in a complete dictionary

conclusion the summing up of an argument, placed at the end of the discussion or discursive text; in general, the end of a process

concrete based on physical objects rather than abstract ideas; compare **abstract**

concrete poem see **shape poem**

conjunction a word that joins parts of sentences: 'and', 'but', 'if', 'although', 'as', 'where'; see also **subordinating conjunction**

connective a word or phrase that links clauses or sentences and signals in which direction the ideas in the sentences are moving. Connectives can indicate, among other things, addition ('also', 'furthermore'), opposition ('however,' 'on the other hand'), reinforcement ('besides', 'after all'), explanation ('for example', 'in other words'), lists ('first', 'finally'), result ('therefore') and time ('meanwhile', 'later').

consonant any letter other than the **vowels**

content the substance of a text, as opposed to its form or style

context the parts of a text immediately before and after the part focused on, which make its precise meaning clear; looking at the context (that is, the rest of the sentence or passage) can often help you work out the meaning of a difficult word. Context is also the background to a text, which may include the effect of the place and time in which the author lived.

contraction the shortening of a word or words: 'she'll' is a contraction of 'she will'. When a word is contracted we use an **apostrophe** to indicate the omitted letters.

copy the written matter in a newspaper or magazine, as opposed to graphics or illustrations

crisis the critical point, or climax, of a story, which the plot has been building up to

criteria standards by which a piece of work is judged and graded

critical analysis a way of analysing literature and commenting on it using technical terms

critical reader someone who reads a text in an active and critical way, searching for meaning and looking at what is both good and bad

cursive joined up (handwriting)

debate a formal discussion in which opposing views are expressed and a vote is taken at the end

description an account or picture of something in words. Descriptions are written in the present tense, and although they must be clear they can use powerful adjectives and verbs to make the description vivid and effective.

device a trick or a technique used by a writer to create a particular effect; see also **narrative device**

dialect a variety of English, often based on region, which has distinctive grammar and vocabulary. Compare **accent**.

dialogue a conversation between two people, which may be spoken or written. Dialogue can refer to the words that the characters speak in a play.

director the person in charge of a production of a play or film. The director is concerned not only with how the words should be spoken and how the characters move and act, but also with how the costumes, lighting and scenery contribute to the overall purpose and effect of the play.

direct speech a way of writing down speech which uses the actual words spoken, e.g. '"I'm tired," said Dave.' Compare **indirect speech**.

discursive text a text that presents argument and information from differing viewpoints. Discursive texts usually use the present tense and logical connectives and make clear the viewpoint expressed at every stage.

display advert an advertisement for a product, often with photographs and graphics, which is placed in a newspaper or magazine by a business

draft to produce an early version of a piece of written work. A text can be developed through a number of drafts before reaching its final version; this drafting process allows improvements and additions to be made and mistakes to be corrected.

drama a performance, or the type of literature intended for performance. Drama is associated not only with the theatre, but also with television, radio and film.

dramatic irony the effect created in a play when the audience knows what is really going on but one or more of the characters does not

dramatic technique a way of making a playscript dramatic or exciting, such as adding a moment of tension, or creating a change of mood or pace

editorial an article in a newspaper which gives the opinion of the editor

election briefing a weighing up of political parties' policies prior to an election

elegy a sad poem or song about someone who has died

emotive designed to create emotion in the audience

entertain to keep someone or an audience interested or amused. Good fiction, for example, uses a variety of narrative devices to entertain its readers.

epitaph the words inscribed on a tombstone

etymological dictionary a dictionary that explains the origins of words

etymology an account of the origins and development of words; also, the derivation of a particular word

evaluate to weigh up how useful something is in the light of the task being set; also, an examination term which requires you to write about the strengths and weaknesses of a subject

evaluation an assessment of the strengths and weaknesses of something

evaluation grid a grid which helps you to evaluate something, for example a text or performance, by analysing its different parts or features

evidence information stated in support of a particular claim or argument; in general, anything that you see, read or are told that gives you reason to believe something

explanation text a text written to explain how or why something happens or is the case. Explanation texts develop ideas logically, use clear, descriptive writing and connectives expressing cause and effect, and are written in impersonal language in the present tense.

explore to investigate thoroughly. An explorer is someone who travels into undiscovered territory to find out more about it.

expression showing your ideas or feelings through your words, tone, gestures or actions

fable a traditional tale, often involving the supernatural, whose purpose is to convey a moral lesson

fact a piece of information which is true; compare **opinion**

factual based on facts and information rather than opinions and assumptions

farce a humorous play or scenario in which ridiculous and unlikely situations occur

feature article an article in a newspaper or magazine that covers a topic in an extensive and interesting way

fiction literature, especially novels and stories, that describes imaginary events and people. Sometimes, however, the setting may be a real place, or the story may be based on a real character or historical event.

figurative language the use of words or expressions in an abstract or imaginative way to create a particular impression or mood. Imagery such as **metaphors**, **similes** and **personification** are examples of figurative language.

first person a way of describing a text in which the writer or speaker refers to himself or herself by using the pronouns 'I' and 'we'; compare **second person**, **third person**

font a style of printing type

formal language language that pays careful attention to Standard English. Formal language may make use of specialist terms and contain many sentences in the passive; it generally avoids slang, colloquialisms and contractions. Compare **informal language**.

free verse verse that has neither rhyme nor a regular rhythm

freeze frame an important moment in a play captured like a photograph to underline its significance

GCSE General Certificate of Secondary Education

gender a way of categorizing nouns by the sex of the thing referred to, i.e. as masculine, feminine or neuter

genre term used to refer to different **text types**, such as narrative, recount and explanation. Genre also means a kind or style of art or literature, which has its own specific features. Comedy, tragedy and satire are genres of drama; genres of novels include horror, romance and science fiction. Genre can also refer to categories of writing, such as poetry, novels and drama.

glossary an alphabetical list of specialist terms with their definitions

grammar the rules of a language, which describe how words can be combined to form phrases, clauses and sentences

haiku a Japanese form of poetry. Haikus usually have three lines with 17 syllables in the pattern 5, 7, 5.

headword a word forming the heading of an entry in a dictionary or encyclopaedia. The headword of the next entry, for example, is 'helper verb'.

helper verb see **auxiliary verb**

home page the opening page of a **website**

homophone a word that sounds the same as another but has a different spelling and meaning: 'right' and 'write'

hot link a word or phrase that can be selected to link users to another part of the website, or to a different website

hypertext multimedia; a type of text that can form links to other texts

iambic pentameter a verse line consisting of five iambs, or metrical feet, each having a short syllable followed by a long syllable

identify to name something

imagery the use of language to create a vivid image or picture. **Metaphor**, **simile** and **personification** are forms of imagery.

imagine to form a picture in your mind of something. Using your imagination can help you to understand what it would be like to be someone or somewhere else.

imperative the form of a verb used to give a command

impersonal writing that uses the third person (he, she or it) is described as impersonal; 'I' is not used

improvise to compose a scene with little planning, or as you perform it

index an alphabetical list of items, usually found at the back of a book

indirect speech (also known as reported speech) a way of writing down speech where the words are referred to indirectly: 'Dave said he was tired.' Compare **direct speech**.

infer reach a conclusion from evidence, deduce

informal language language that includes **colloquial** language, **slang** and the use of **contracted** forms of words: 'Don't you eat no poison berries.' Compare **formal language**.

information text a text written to inform. Information texts use the present tense and the third person, make clear how the information is organized and linked, and often incorporate examples.

instruction text a text written to help readers achieve certain goals, especially how to make or do something. Instruction texts generally include a statement of the goal ('How to make a sponge cake') and follow a sequence of steps in chronological order to achieve the goal ('Then cream the sugar and butter'). Imperative verbs are used, and connectives often refer to the order in which the various steps are to be taken ('First…', 'Next…').

interactive responding to the input of the user

interpret to present a piece of writing or music so that a particular meaning is given to it

introduction the opening section of a text which sets the scene or explains what is to follow

inverted comma a punctuation mark used to show the beginning and end of direct speech or to highlight a particular word ('Look out!' said Dave) (the word 'genuine'). Inverted commas are also known as quotation marks.

irony a type of humour in which words are used to imply the opposite of what they normally mean

jingle a short catchy phrase or rhyme set to music and used to advertise something on radio or television

key sentence the most important sentence in a paragraph

Key Stage 3 the term given to the first three years of secondary school in England, Wales and Northern Ireland

KWL grid a grid to structure your research thinking for a research project, which asks you what you already Know, what you Want to know, and what you have Learnt at the end of the project

Latin the language of the Romans, which provides the roots for thousands of English words and place names

layout the way a text is presented on the page

lead article the main article on a newspaper or magazine page

lead character the main character in a story or play

lead item the main item that begins a television or radio news programme

lead story the main plot, especially in a soap opera; also, the lead article

limerick a five-line comic verse made famous by a writer called Edward Lear. The first, second and fifth lines of a limerick are long, and the third and fourth lines are short; it follows the rhyming scheme a a b b a.

listings a list of concerts, films and other events printed in a newspaper or magazine

literacy reading and writing skill

literary non-fiction text based on real events in people's lives, such as biographies, autobiographies, diaries and letters

logical following a reasonable, well thought out, step-by-step approach, where the connections between each step are made clear

lyric poem a poem that focuses on an important moment in the poet's life, and is concerned with the emotions evoked by that event

magic e a spelling rule: if you add an 'e' onto a consonant-vowel-consonant (CVC) word, such as 'fat', the short vowel sound is turned into the long vowel sound ('fate'). In other words, adding 'e' to CVC words makes the vowel say its own name. The same is true of CCVC words, such as 'plan'.

masthead the title of a newspaper and accompanying logos that identify it

memoir an autobiographical record

metaphor a form of **imagery** when one thing is said to be another: 'You are my sun and my moon'

Metaphysical poets a group of 17th-century poets whose poems tended to be in the form of a dramatic argument, often using outrageous logic

metre the way in which words and syllables are arranged in poetry or music to create a regular rhythm

mnemonic a strategy or method of remembering something: 'There is a rat in separate'

modal verb a type of auxiliary (or 'helper') verb which expresses possibility (can, might), speculation (could, might), permission (can, may), obligation (ought, should) or necessity (should, must)

monologue a speech made directly to the audience which reveals a character's inner thoughts

moral a short moral lesson at the end of a **fable**

morphology the consistent patterns of letters that make up words

multiple narration using an autobiographical style but telling the same story through the eyes of two or more narrators who have differing perspectives (e.g. the new student, a student who victimizes them, the class teacher)

myth an ancient story of gods or heroes which attempts to explain events or human nature

narrative a text which retells events, often in chronological sequence. Narrative texts may be fictional or non-fiction.

narrative device a trick used by an author to make their writing interesting and entertaining, such as the use of imagery, repetition and descriptive language

narrative perspective the point of view from which a story is written; compare **narrative voice**

narrative poem a poem that tells a story. Earlier narrative poems, called ballads, have short, regular verses with a rhyme scheme

narrative voice the 'person' that a writer uses to narrate a story: the two main narrative voices are **first person** (using 'I' and 'me') and **third person** (using 'he/she'); compare **narrative perspective**

navigable structured so that you can find your way around the text easily

navigate to find your way around a text

NC level National Curriculum level – a grade between 1 and 8 which is given to your work. The average standard which is expected of students in Year 9 NCTs is to achieve level 5 or 6.

NCT National Curriculum Test. All students in England and Wales are expected to take NCTs in English, maths and science in Years 2, 6 and 9.

neutral see **unbiased**

non-fiction any form of text that is not **fiction**

non-Standard English written or spoken language that is informal or in a dialect; compare **Standard English**

noun a word that names an object or quality: 'dog', 'luck', 'Birmingham'

noun phrase a wider term than 'noun'. It often refers to a group of words in a sentence that functions in the same way as a noun: 'all the colours of the rainbow'. It can also refer to a single noun or pronoun.

object the person or thing being acted upon in a sentence: 'Winston scored a goal', 'We visited the Millennium Dome.' Compare **subject**.

objective based on fact and reason, unbiased, not influenced by personal feelings; compare **subjective**

OHP overhead projector

OHT a transparency used to display text on an overhead projector

omniscient author a narrative voice in which an author writes from the godlike perspective of knowing everything about the characters' innermost thoughts and feelings as well as all the events of the story

onomatopoeia the effect created by words which copy the sounds associated with their meaning: 'crack', 'hiss', 'murmur', 'quack'

open question a question designed to get as much information as possible; compare **closed question**

opinion a belief or view about something or someone; compare **fact**

opinion piece an article in a newspaper which presents a personal view on an important issue

oral to do with speaking rather than writing; compare **aural**

oral tradition the way in which traditional stories are handed down from one generation to the next by word of mouth; such stories are not written down until later

overmatter copy that has been typeset but that cannot be used for printing owing to lack of space

paragraph a section of a piece of writing, used to organize the argument or help readers follow the storyline. A new paragraph should mark a new topic or a change of focus; in dialogue paragraphs mark a change of speaker.

parody a composition which mimics the style of another author in a humorous way

Glossary

participle a form of the verb that can help to form a clause. Present participles are formed by adding '-ing' to the base form of regular verbs: 'needing', 'helping'. Past participles are formed by adding '-ed' to the base form of regular verbs: 'needed', 'helped'; many are irregular and have other endings: 'flown', 'kept', 'written'.

passive the 'voice' used when the subject of a sentence is acted upon by the verb: 'The man was arrested.' Passive sentences tell you what happened and who it happened to but they do not usually tell you who or what performed the action. Compare 'The man was arrested' (passive) with 'The police arrested the man' (**active**).

performance a live entertainment provided for an audience

person a way of classifying pronouns and verb forms according to whether they indicate the speaker (**first person**), the person addressed (**second person**) or someone else (**third person**)

persona a character or role taken on by someone

personification a form of **imagery** when an inanimate object is described in language that relates to animals or humans: 'the tree whispered', 'the bicycle shivered'

persuasive text a text which aims to persuade the reader or listener to accept a point of view. Persuasive texts often contain reasons and evidence, use logical connectives and a range of devices to appeal to their audience, such as emphasizing key points and using emotive words.

phrase a group of words, which only makes full sense as part of a sentence. There can be **noun phrases** ('his best book'), adjectival phrases ('not bad') and **adverbial phrases** ('six hours later').

plan to decide in detail what something is going to be and how to do it

planning frame a grid that helps you plan your writing or presentation

playscript the text of a play, which includes the dialogue, stage directions and notes on the setting; also called the script

plot the storyline of a novel or play; compare **theme**

plural the form of a word that is used to refer to two or more people or things. 'Trees' and 'taxes' are plural nouns; 'they were late' includes a plural pronoun and plural verb. Compare **singular**.

polemic a controversial discussion

portmanteau word a word formed by running together or blending two words: 'smog' from 'smoke' + 'fog'

preface introduction to a text explaining its scope and intention

prefix a group of letters that can be added to the beginning of a word to change its meaning or function: 'unknown', 'extraordinary', 'international'. Other prefixes are 'in', 'dis', 'super', 're' and 'micro'.

preposition a word that shows how one thing is related to another: 'above the bed', 'to the town', 'with Gavin'

present formally put forward an idea or piece of dramatic, spoken or written work to somebody

presentation a piece of dramatic, spoken or written work that is formally presented to an audience; also, the way in which a piece of written work is laid out on the page or on screen

producer the person responsible for the production of a television or radio programme

prologue introductory lines to a play, speech or text

pronoun a word used to replace a noun, a noun phrase or a clause, in order to avoid repetition. 'I', 'you', 'we', 'its', 'herself', 'this', 'that', 'who', 'which' and 'what' are some of the many pronouns.

proof a print-out of text made so that errors can be corrected

proofread to check the final draft of a text carefully for mistakes

protagonist the main character in a play or story

punctuation a way of marking text with symbols (punctuation marks) to help readers' understanding. The most common punctuation marks are: apostrophe, bracket, colon, comma, dash, exclamation mark, full stop, hyphen, inverted comma (speech mark), question mark and semi-colon.

purpose the reason for something, for example the reason why a text is written

qualify to alter the meaning of a word, phrase or sentence by adding a word, often an adverb: in the sentence 'The water's fairly hot', the adverb 'fairly' qualifies the word 'hot'

quotation a phrase or passage that is repeated in another text to give evidence of something or to support a particular view. Short quotations are usually put inside inverted commas in the main body of the text; longer quotations are usually set off from the text, with a space above and below, and don't use inverted commas.

quotation mark see **inverted comma**

rap poem a form of oral poetry, associated with Caribbean and Afro-Caribbean cultures, which has a strong rhythm and rapid pace

recount a text written to be retold for information or entertainment. Recount texts may be fiction, in which the language is descriptive and there may be dialogue; or non-fiction, which generally retell events in chronological order, in the past tense, and use connectives that signal time.

reference text an information text organized in a clearly defined way (such as alphabetically) and used to research facts and data. Encyclopaedias and dictionaries are examples of reference texts.

register the level of formality of language used, such as colloquial, formal, official etc

repetition repeating a word, phrase or sentence for a particular effect. Repetition is a common feature of persuasive texts; it can also have an emotive effect in poetry: 'Break, break, break,/ On thy cold grey stones, O Sea!'

report a text written to describe or classify, such as a guide book or a report on a school trip. Report texts often begin with a general classification, then describe particular characteristics and end with a summary. See **information text**.

reportage a text – often in the form of diaries or letters – that reports significant events in the world as or soon after they happen. Reportage is characterized by a sense of immediacy, because the writer is an eyewitness who was either a close observer of, or a participant in, the events being described.

reported speech see **indirect speech**

reporting clause the clause that shows who speaks the words in **direct speech**, and sometimes how they speak them

reservation something added to a statement to make it less strong

resolution the resolving of the crisis, tension or other problem in a scene

review to write an account expressing your opinion of a book, play or film; also the account itself. Review also means to look again at something, such as a piece of work, and think about how effective it is and whether it could be improved.

rhetoric the art of effective or persuasive speaking or writing; also, language designed to persuade or impress

rhetorical devices techniques used to persuade an audience or reader

rhetorical question a question that doesn't require an answer: 'Am I going to take this lying down?' Rhetorical questions are often asked for dramatic or persuasive effect.

rhyme a pattern that occurs when words or the endings of words share the same sound, especially in verse. Rhymes usually occur at the end of lines, but internal rhyme can also take place: 'Who made bats and cats and rats?'

rhyme scheme the way rhyming words are organized in a poem. When writing out a rhyme scheme you usually use different letters for each line, but the same letter if two lines rhyme. For example, '… cars/… knives/… guns/… lives' has the rhyme scheme ABCB.

rhythm a regular pattern of sound created by the choice and arrangement of words, especially in verse. The pattern is made by the alternation of light and heavy beats (or **stresses**). **Blank verse**, for example, has a regular pattern of ten syllables with five stresses in each line: 'For he to-day that sheds his blood with me'.

ridicule making fun of an opinion so as to make it appear wrong or stupid. Ridicule is a device used in some persuasive texts.

role play an exercise in which people act the part of another character

Roman alphabet the alphabet, developed by the ancient Romans, that is used for writing most of the languages of western Europe and many other languages

Romantic poets poets writing in the period from about 1789 to 1832, such as Coleridge or Wordsworth, who brought a new level of emotional intensity and imagination to their work

root see **stem**

sarcasm when you say or do the opposite of what you really mean in order to mock or insult someone

scan to look over a text very quickly in order to find information by locating a key word; compare **skim**

scenario situation

script see **playscript**

search engine a service provided on the internet which allows users to search for items of interest

second person a way of describing a text in which the writer or speaker refers to the reader or audience by using the pronoun 'you'; compare **first person**, **third person**

Glossary

sentence a group of words that makes sense. Sentences usually have a subject and a verb, begin with a capital letter and end with a full stop (or exclamation mark or question mark).

sequence to put into a logical order

setting the place and time in which a story or drama is set

shape poem a poem in which the layout of the words reflects the subject, or an aspect of the subject. Also called concrete poem.

simile a form of **imagery** when one thing is compared to another: 'His face was like a wrinkled prune', 'She was as happy as a lark'

simple sentence a sentence containing only one **clause**: 'Salman took the bus'

singular referring to one thing or person. 'Tree' and 'tax' are singular nouns; 'was' and 'runs' are singular verbs. Compare **plural**.

sketch a short piece of humorous drama, usually part of a comedy show

skim to read a passage quickly in order to get an overview of its subject matter and main ideas; compare **scan**

slang words and phrases that are used in informal contexts, and often by particular groups of people, such as schoolchildren

slapstick comedy characterized by physical, knockabout action

soap opera a serial drama which is broadcast in frequent episodes on television or radio. Soap operas focus on the lives of people living or working in a particular place, and have many different subplots.

soliloquy a speech in a play when a character is alone and speaks their thoughts aloud

sonnet a poem with 14 lines, often in two stanzas of eight lines then six lines. Sonnets follow a variety of rhyme schemes.

sound bite information that is packaged in a few words so that it fits nicely into very short interviews

source a text or document that provides evidence; also, a text used by an author to help them in their own writing

specialist dictionary a dictionary which gives the highly technical terms relating to specialized study

spell-checker a computer program which checks the spelling of words in a file

spelling log a book in which the student records words that he or she finds difficult to spell, and that offers strategies to improve spelling

spiritual a Black American religious song

spokesperson someone who speaks on behalf of a group, for example by stating the group's findings in an activity

spoof a mildly satirical mockery or parody

stage direction direction given to actors in the **playscript** as to how to say their lines and how to move on stage

Standard English the type of spoken and written English that should be used when formal language is appropriate. Standard English is the language spoken and written by the majority of educated speakers of English and taught in schools.

stanza a verse; a group of lines with a particular pattern, which is repeated throughout the poem

stem the root or main part of a word, which remains unchanged whatever its tense or number etc.: the stem of 'recount', 'counted' and 'counting' is 'count'

storyline the **plot** of a novel or short story

strapline additional text that accompanies a newspaper headline

stream of consciousness telling all the thoughts inside someone's head in an autobiographical style

stress the emphasis put on particular words, or on certain syllables or parts of words. For example, 'reflected' is stressed on the second syllable, 'flec'.

structure the way a text is arranged and organized

style the language features of a text; the way in which a text is written, spoken or performed

subject the person or thing performing the action of the sentence: '<u>Rachel</u> scored a hat-trick', 'The <u>Millennium Dome</u> was a flop.' Compare **object**.

subjective influenced by personal feelings and opinion, **biased**

subordinate clause a clause that adds information to, or qualifies, the main clause of a sentence: '<u>If you get home late</u>, you'll miss the programme'; 'I spoke to Dad, <u>who was very helpful</u>.' Subordinate clauses cannot exist on their own, but are dependent on the main clause or another subordinate clause.

subordinating conjunction a word or phrase such as 'when', 'although', 'before', 'until', 'where', 'like', 'as', 'because', 'since', 'so that', 'in order to' and 'if' which introduces a **subordinate clause**: 'I spoke to Dad <u>when</u> I got home'

subplot a storyline that runs alongside the main **plot** of a play or story, which contrasts with or throws light on the main action

subtext a message which is not stated directly but hinted at in some way; also, an underlying theme in a piece of writing

suffix a group of letters that can be added to the end of a word to change its meaning or function: 'break<u>able</u>', 'post<u>ed</u>', 'fine<u>st</u>'. Other suffixes are 'ly', 's', 'er', 'ward' and 'ful'.

suspense a state of excited expectation produced in an audience; a dramatic or narrative technique used by writers

syllable a beat in a word, usually consisting of a vowel sound with one or more consonants before or after. There are two syllables in 'river' and one syllable in 'bridge'.

synonym a word with roughly the same meaning as another word. Lists of synonyms are collected in a **thesaurus**. Compare **antonym**.

synopsis summary

syntax the grammatical rules of a language; also, the way in which words and phrases are arranged to form sentences relating

tabloid a smaller format newspaper; compare **broadsheet**

target what you are aiming to achieve; see also **attainment target**

tense the way a verb shows whether it is referring to the past ('looked', 'have looked', 'had looked'), the present ('look') or the future ('will look')

text the name given to a block of language which has been written or spoken in order to communicate something

text type a type of writing; a way of categorizing texts that share similar features. Information texts and explanation texts, for example, are two different text types.

theme the subject or underlying idea of a piece of writing, for example the triumph of good over evil, or how the world of the spirit is closer to the real world than we think; compare **plot**

thesaurus a book containing lists of **synonyms**, words which are similar in meaning. Thesauruses can help you to vary words that are used frequently (such as 'said'), and to select the word with the precise shade of meaning that you require.

third person a way of describing a text in which the writer or speaker refers to somebody or something else ('s/he', 'it', 'they', 'Harry'); compare **first person**, **second person**

title sequence the opening shots of a television programme which give the programme's title and set the mood

tone particular quality or style; atmosphere

transcript a written version of something that is spoken

type see **text type**

unbiased not favouring one side or argument over another, balanced, impartial, even-handed

understatement a statement that, for effect, doesn't say fully how true something is, for example 'I was not impressed' when actually the speaker or writer was appalled

unseen text an examination term that refers to a text that you haven't read before, to which you must respond and demonstrate understanding

verb a word that describes an action, a happening, a process or a state; a 'doing' or 'being' word 'go', 'want', 'is', 'feel'. Verbs change their form according to the **tense** and the **person** attached to them.

voice see **active** and **passive**; see also **narrative voice**

vowel any of the letters 'a', 'e', 'i', 'o' or 'u'; compare **consonant**

weasel words words that are deliberately misleading, in order to persuade someone to do or feel something

website a group of connected pages on the World Wide Web containing information on a particular subject

whiteboard a wipeable board which may be used by teachers to demonstrate teaching points and by students to record responses

wit the ability to use words and ideas in an amusing and clever way

word class a way of classifying words with the same function. The main word classes are verb, noun, adjective, adverb, pronoun, determiner, preposition and conjunction. Word classes are also called 'parts of speech'.

writing frame a grid that supports your writing by providing the opening phrases of paragraphs